Other Great Brand Stories

Adidas *All Day I Dream About Sport: The story of the adidas brand* by Conrad Brunner

Arsenal *Winning Together: The story of the Arsenal brand* by John Simmons & Matt Simmons

Banyan Tree *A Brand Born of Romance* by Andy Milligan

Beckham *The Story of How Brand Beckham was Built* by Andy Milligan

eBay *The Story of a Brand that Taught Millions of People to Trust One Another* by Elen Lewis

Google *Search Me: The surprising success of Google* by Neil Taylor

Guinness *Guinness is Guinness: The colourful story of a black and white brand* by Mark Griffiths

Harry Potter *Wizard!: Harry Potter's brand magic* by Stephen Brown

Ikea *A Brand for All the People* by Elen Lewis

Innocent *Building a Brand from Nothing but Fruit* by John Simmons

Scotch Whisky *Creative Fire: The story of Scotland's greatest export* by Stuart Delves

Starbucks *My Sister's a Barista: How they made Starbucks a home away from home* by John Simmons

United States *Brand America: The mother of all brands* by Simon Anholt & Jeremy Hildreth

Great Brand Stories
Dyson

The domestic engineer: How Dyson changed the meaning of cleaning

Iain Carruthers

Copyright © 2007 Iain Carruthers

First published in 2007 by Cyan Books, an imprint of

Cyan Communications Limited
119 Wardour Street
London W1F 0UW
United Kingdom
T +44 (0)20 7565 6120
sales@cyanbooks.com
www.cyanbooks.com

The right of Iain Carruthers to be identified as the author
of this work has been asserted by him in accordance
with the Copyright, Designs and Patents Act 1988.

A CIP record for this book is available from the British Library

ISBN-13 978-1-904879-79-4
ISBN-10 1-904879-79-9

Designed by Rick Sellars
With thanks to Dyson for the photographs

Printed and bound in Great Britain by
TJ International Ltd, Padstow, Cornwall

For Mia and Kate. This is all about Mr Dynamite.

Acknowledgments

Many people have helped me in putting this together. I'd particularly like to thank those who gave of their time and insight: Jeffre Jackson (www.pinkair.com), Russell Davies (www.russelldavies.com) and Bill Critchley, the late Alan Fletcher, John Kearon of BrainJuicer, Malcolm Evans and Fiona McNae of Space Doctors, and Graham Capron-Tee—as well as those who preferred not to be named, within and outwith Dyson.

At Dyson, I'd particularly like to thank Kirsten Gower, (and, later, Lucy Grimster and Guy Lambert) who shepherded me through the organization, as well as my interviewees there—service teams, engineers and executives.

At Cyan, Martin Liu, Pom Somkabcharti and Rick Sellars have been responsive and inventive in equal measure. Thank you.

Contents

Preface

Dyson is one of those brands that would rather not be called a brand. It feels more comfortable in being a product or a number of products. It has marketing managers who deny the b-word's existence in the Dyson lexicon. But a brand exists in someone else's head, so struggle against the notion as those managers might, the Dyson brand pulses powerfully inside the heads of millions of people worldwide. And, of course, Dyson makes great products.

There is a philosophical debate that is threaded through this book. What is a brand? Is the brand "he", "it" or "they"? Here is a brand, product, company built around the personality and work of one man—isn't it, isn't he, aren't they? Business is often seen differently if you change one simple pronoun. People have been too ready to dehumanize business life and turn it into a corporate undertaking. Iain Carruthers believes that's a grave mistake. And so, I suspect, does James Dyson.

So, to reassert the vital human credentials of business life, Iain Carruthers is happy to demonstrate that brands are about stories. The Dyson story, and the purity of attitude that James Dyson himself embodies, is a challenge for anyone who works in branding. It is an archetypal story in itself, about an engineer who strives ambitiously for perfection. Any number of Greek myths spring to mind but Dyson himself is determinedly unheroic.

Iain Carruthers tells the story well. He connects the contemporary world of marketing with the archetypal world of storytelling. Cutting-edge research techniques encounter the narrative theory of Joseph Campbell. It makes for a heady brew, one that stimulates rather than sedates. As you read, questions are raised, to explore the central question of the debate: what is a brand? This question is the book's narrative impulse. The story develops by pursuing that question and others that spring from it, such as why do we invent brands, and how can they be used to disguise indifferent products as well as to illuminate great ones. By the end, you are content to form your own answers. It's an enjoyable pursuit.

John Simmons
Series editor, *Great brand stories*

"We live either affirming or denying what makes us most original."

R. D. Laing

Chapter 1
Domestic Engineering

"Dyson.
Oh really?
We've got
dozens of
them around
the palace."

Her Majesty Queen Elizabeth II

On a clear November's day, I step out of a taxi at Dyson's headquarters at Malmesbury in Wiltshire.

On the approach, there's no clear sign that this is Dyson. The building is set off the road. Only as you come up to the security gate does the anonymity dissolve and do you begin to see the low swoop of the architecture. The building is strong, almost squat, despite the curves and sails of the roof. It is almost military in its cleanness.

The taxi driver, who had been holding forth on the virtues of the company and "James" paused as he drew up. "Mind you, I don't hold with those."

"Those" are a series of abstract nude sculptures on the external pathways and cleaving to the side of the buildings. They man the outside, silent sentinels.

The car park is full. I notice only one empty space near the building. It's marked JD. I don't see any other marked spaces.

You reach reception. It's an airy space, dwarfing the receptionist on the left-hand side. Display cases house the icons of the business. The washing machines sit in grey and purple splendour. The main feature, hugging the steel staircase, is an array of upright vacuum cleaners, charting the evolution of the main product. Underneath my feet are glass sections with other products glittering up at you. Icons, everywhere. There are no newspapers or handouts. Just two copies of a magazine describing luxury brands, with Dyson nestling in among the grand hotels and the Wedgwood. Discreet signage makes it clear to the visitor this isn't so much the headquarters as the Dyson Research and Development Building.

I'm always intrigued, when I visit organizations, by what they show you first. Here, I'm led to the testing labs, or at least those bits I'm allowed to see. Within minutes of my visit, I'm in the research and testing centre.

Organizations often have a metaphor by which they live, consciously or unconsciously. Dyson's is up there for display. We're engineers. We're interested in why things work—and why they don't.

Sitting in reception and then wandering through the building, you are struck by the youthfulness of the place and its people. There is a casual intensity when people work. Listen closely and you hear a sort of purposeful hum.

It's engrossing. It's seductive.

This book is a treasure hunt. I'm delighted you're accompanying me. We're going to follow a number of pathways, each of which has a chapter. Each chapter contains clues as to the purpose and power of the Dyson business, but also ranges more widely. The great thing about this organization is that it enables us to look at some very juicy topics: how a business grows; the role of product design; how innovation does—and doesn't—work. Our reward is to understand how this fits together, and what it tells us about contemporary business.

The grit in the oyster is that this is a book in a series called *Great brand stories*, yet Dyson doesn't think of itself as a brand. It is a construct it either doesn't believe in, or with which it doesn't want to be associated.

It is not alone here. Some very strong "brands" don't hold with the idea of branding, both because the term has become pejorative and because it implies a preoccupation with managing and manipulating opinion, rather than just projecting what you believe and want to sell. Interbrand, my former employer, published a book called *The Future of Brands* in 2000, in which some of the most engaging quotes were from companies rather uncomfortable with the idea of branding, despite their status as international brands, and, therefore, with their inclusion in the book.

So Dyson's refusal to acknowledge that it is a brand could be an unwillingness to engage in the conventional games of marketing. Or a self-conceit: as one of my interviewees put it, an engineer pretending not to be a marketer is a very good marketing strategy. We'll see.

Before we get started we should get acquainted with the main thrust of the Dyson narrative. A few salient points.

What's the company about?

Dyson is a UK-based, international business, with most of its production located in Malaysia. Its main products are vacuum cleaners. The company has been, by any standards, remarkably successful, gaining significant market shares in the UK, Australia, Western Europe, and, in recent years, the US. It also makes washing machines, though that, as we shall see, has been more problematic.

Who's James Dyson?

He's an industrial designer and engineer, who, before founding the business that bears his name, designed and manufactured several other successful products, including a military transport boat and a superior wheelbarrow called the Ballbarrow. His original intent was not to make and sell the vacuum cleaners, but to license the cyclone technology to others, allowing him to continue to design and innovate in other areas.

What do you mean "cyclone technology"?

Good question. What makes a Dyson different is the way it continues to work well even when you've vacuumed a few times. This is what they mean by "no loss of suction" a phrase that at Dyson is not so much a slogan as a mantra— you'll probably find it tattooed on the buttocks of long-serving employees.

Dysons and conventional vacuums create suction in the same way. A motorized fan spins, expelling air from the machine, creating that familiar nasal whine and a strong inflowing current of air. You train that current onto a surface, and it lifts dust and dirt. That's the easy bit. The important thing is what happens to the muck as it flows back in: you have to separate the air from the dust, otherwise you're just left with a cargo of air-borne garbage.

With conventional vacuuming, this happens by the dust being filtered through a bag, the air passing through and the dust remaining. The bag's pores get clogged up pretty quickly, slowing the current and making the whole thing less efficient.

With a Dyson, the current of air and dust gets pulled into a cone shaped cylinder. When they hit the curve of the cylinder wall, the air and dust particles radically increase their speed, and do so again as they hit the next curve of the cylinder. A dust particle enters the vacuum at 20mph and ends up at 1,000mph. This creates a relatively huge g-force on the particles and they promptly surrender, being forced to the bottom of the plastic bin, and growing into that grey fluff familiar to owners of the brand. Dust is literally spun out of the air.

So a Dyson doesn't suck any differently. It just has a smart way of clearing out the dust so that it can continue to work properly. I think it's good we got that out of the way.

Let's start with some history.

A very British invention

> **"I was bowing down in front of Her Majesty to receive this great big medal around my neck (a CBE) when she said, 'And what do you do, Mr Dyson?' I told her that I was the manufacturer of the Dyson**

> **vacuum cleaner. 'Oh really?'**
> **she said. We've got dozens**
> **of them around the palace."**
> James Dyson, *Against the Odds*

All rather fitting, since her ancestor, King Edward VII was the very first owner of a vacuum cleaner. It came about like this.

In 1901, a London engineer called H. Cecil Booth was invited to a demonstration at the Empire Music Hall of a "machine for the mechanical removal of dust." It was a rather complex machine that involved blowing compressed air at a carpet and trying to collect the resultant dust in a box. Booth thought the American inventor seemed to be "going round three sides of a house to get across the front" so he suggested that a suction method might be appropriate. He got a frosty reception, but went off to experiment on his own. [1]

> **"I thought over the matter for**
> **a few days and tried the experiment**
> **of sucking (through a handkerchief)**
> **with my mouth against the back**
> **of a plush seat in a restaurant in**
> **Victoria Street with the result that**
> **I was almost choked."**

On recovering, Booth saw that the underside of the handkerchief was thick with dust. Armed with this insight and some development cash, he developed an unwieldy but effective horsedrawn monster powered by an internal combustion engine. The Puffing Billy, as it became known, parked outside a venue and a gang of men with long hoses

came in to do the business. Folklore has it that just before the coronation of Edward VII, the carpet on which the thrones were to stand was filthy. Booth was summoned and the carpet cleaned. He got an order for two from the Royal Household shortly after. His company was named Goblin, a business that remains today.

Two interesting points emerge. First, how long it took for someone to have the insight about suction. Compressed air blowing devices had been around for sometime, such as the "Whirlwind," invented in Chicago in the 1860s. It takes a long time for the apparently obvious to happen. We are held captive by our assumptions about how things should be, which we'll see later when we examine James Dyson's fruitless attempts to persuade the late 20th century appliance industry of the virtues of a product that would, some years later, comprehensively eat their lunch.

Second, we discover how profoundly dirty Victorian England was. Booth had had first-hand experience of this over his lunch in Victoria, but that was only a taster. His machines took half a ton of dust and dirt out of the carpets and fittings of a West End department store in one night. After four weeks work at the Crystal Palace, 26 tons of dust were carried off. The industrial age had many consequences, and dirt was one of them: dust and fumes spewed from engines and factories; skin mites dropped from the millions of people who migrated to towns and cities. In 1910, Professor Stanley Kent of University College Bristol found 355,500,000 living organisms in just one gramme of dust extracted from Marlborough House, the home of HRH The Princess of Wales. Those royals again. [2]

Did that last bit make you feel a bit itchy?

You can see why vacuums are such a good business. Their great selling point, then and now, is the provocation of human disgust. We have evolved an acute sensitivity to smells, sights and tastes that we believe are toxic to us. We are intimate with bacteria, bugs, dirt and dust daily. But we don't want to know this. We therefore revel in their removal from our bodies, our clothes and our homes. We want them excluded, physically and psychologically.

My mother-in-law used to have a part time job as a saleswoman for Electrolux. Betty's pitch was to shake out dirt on a piece of carpet and then remove it with the machine. Overtly, this exhibited the cleaning power of an Electrolux. Covertly, the message was, "Madam, your house, and therefore you, are dirtier than you like to think. This sample of dirt, multiplied a thousandfold, is everywhere in your home. Currently, you're not getting it up."

Back to the 1900s. Someone else not getting it up was the splendidly named James Murray Spangler. An asthmatic janitor, in Canton, Ohio, his response to the dust causing him such discomfort was to rig up the first recognizable vacuum cleaner from wood, tin, an electric motor, a broomstick and a pillow case. Not only did he make it usable and mobile, but he also incorporated a bristle brush to loosen debris. Over in San Francisco, Messrs Chapman and Skinner had spent 1905 assembling the first "portable" cleaner but their definition of portability weighed in at 92 pounds. History has little more to say about them.

Like so many inventors, Spangler never really got the full benefit from his ingenuity. His wife's cousin was another resident of Ohio, one W. H. Hoover. Hoover was in the positively filthy business of being a tanner, but he knew a good bet, and he bought the rights. Which means, of course, that generations of Britons have been denied the joy of giving the carpet a quick spangle, or getting the Spangler out.

Hoover remorselessly exploited the invention. His great innovation was commercial, not technical. He took out advertising offering a free trial of the product to those responding to the ad. But rather than sending the machine direct to the customer, he sent it to stores in the areas the letters were coming from, giving a commission to the store manager for a sale. From this, he built the national dealer network that remains the basis of the company's distribution today.

From about 1920 through to the 1980s, vacuum cleaners evolved fitfully. Better bags, more suction, beating brushes, even models with headlights for those awkward spots. Dyson would have you believe that cleaners were little more than motorized sticks with pillow cases attached until they came along, but that's a little fanciful. A lot of things in life don't change that much. Cars are still internal combustion engines with four wheels and a steering wheel.

But change was afoot.

"This poxy machine"

On a rainy afternoon in 1978, an inventor/entrepreneur called James Dyson began to get very annoyed with the anaemic performance of his Hoover Junior. By repeated disembowellings of the machine and its dustbag, he established that the basic ability of the machine to suck was persistently compromised by the clogging up of the bag. It was, in his words, crap. By chance, he soon after encountered a dust removing mechanism called a cyclone, which span dust from the air using centrifugal force, rather than trying to push it through a paper bag. He collided the experiences together, developing a small scale cyclone that could remedy the gaping deficiencies of his poxy machine at home. Over the next three years, in a backyard building, the cyclone evolved.

Every business or organization has its origin myth. I use myth in the technical sense: not a fiction, but a story designed to carry meaning. Hewlett and Packard tinkered in their garage, making electronic testing equipment. Soichiro Honda assembled makeshift motorbikes in his wooden shack. Business leaders consciously use and adumbrate such myths in order to re-inforce what they believe to be important. The more narcissistic will publish their autobiographies as part of the process: Richard Branson, Jack Welch, Lee Iaccoca, John Harvey Jones.

In business, myths work primarily for employees and investors: they make sense of why we are here and why we do what we do. In the same way, adherents of particular religions or groups have myths. The myths can be used to attract converts or leaked to customers, as a means of establishing authenticity and interest. They act as an anchor point for why you are making a particular choice.

The Dyson origin story is powerful because it carries the seeds of the brand's point of view about the world. In buying a Dyson, you acquire a point of view. That things could and should be better. It's the great rational story of progress. How we tackle and conquer the physical world, and overcome the forces of lethargy and indifference while we do so.

And, in this case, we have a plucky, talented and good-looking hero to carry the narrative.

It's a story we're going to explore in the rest of the book.

Chapter 2
It Either Works or It Doesn't

"Progress,
therefore,
is not an
accident but
a necessity . . .
It is a part
of nature."

Herbert Spencer, *Social Statistics*

Every book is built from a set of data: of research, conversation, impression and opinion. This chapter uses specially commissioned market research to provide a basis for our understanding of Dyson, based on the understanding of representative customers in the vacuum cleaner market. It then goes on to explain why most people are impressed by Dyson without really knowing why.

For the market research, we looked at three key markets. The first is the UK, where the business is located, and where Dyson has the highest market share. The second is Germany, Europe's largest market. And the third is the US, the big kahuna. In each case, we selected a nationally representative group of 18–64 year olds, each of whom had a vacuum cleaner, and were aware of the Dyson name.

We worked with BrainJuicer, one of Europe's fastest growing online research companies, because of its innovative way of capturing and feeding back consumer opinions. Its "Mind Reader" technique mimics the human brain in the way that it builds up impressions and understanding by association.

We understand people, organizations and ideas by collecting and processing impressions of them. Like children building a house of Lego, we select and discard pieces to assemble a picture.

We have conversations in order to make sense of our impressions of the world, and these conversations coalesce around themes. Your understanding of any given topic, while appearing to you to be "your" opinion, is a work in progress, today's update on the conversations the world is having about that topic.

Think, for example, of how people in your immediate or extended family talk about you. "Oh, Jonathan, yes. He's always . . . "Sheila's been like that ever since . . ." Gradually, a myth is built up about you, which is in part comforting, because it helps you understand your identity, and part irritating, because it only represents part of you. Or it may wholly misrepresent you, since it's made up of badly patched together tales of your childhood.

> **"This is family. In the family, you are a certain kind of person. Your mother, my mother in particular, piles one half-truth about your character on another until she has built up a whole structure, a fabricated person. It begins in small ways: you are untidy or reliable or good with figures or you eat too fast; you're frightened of frogs, you hold your pen in the wrong way, and then these threads are woven into the family tapestry, a sort of Bayeux which for ever commemorates this entirely imaginary scene."** [3]
> Justin Cartwright, *The Promise of Happiness*

In other words, as humans, we fabricate each other. This doesn't mean that we lie: we simply assemble, from what we have available, the impressions that are meaningful to us. We are meaning-making machines. Companies rely on this process to sell us things. They fabricate meaning about their products in order to speed the process by which you make sense of them, in their favour.

Mind Reader is an attempt to disaggregate this meaning, to reverse engineer the impressions of a brand or company into their constituent parts. It asks for the three main associations someone has with a topic, and how positive or negative people feel about each association, using a colour scale (here using shades of grey). You are also allowed to endorse others' associations if you agree with them, but you assign your own level of feeling about them.

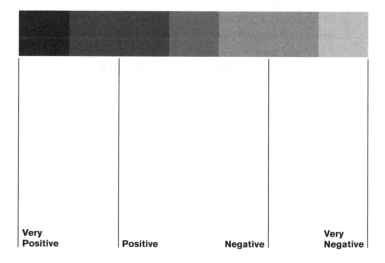

Very Positive   **Positive**   **Negative**   **Very Negative**

For example. If the topic was duvets, your associations might be:

Keeps me warm and snuggly

Sort of French

Awkward to wash and stuff into the quilt cover

Which is as far as most surveys go. But a Mind Reader doesn't rest there. For each of these associations, it then asks you further associations, which is where things get interesting.

Keeps me warm and snuggly

In bed with my wife

Good for wrapping up little children and carrying around when playing

Part of being intimate

Which gets to the real issues of duvets and helps the duvet marketeer—if there is such a creature—to understand what kind of meaning-making is going on around their product.

Dyson and Mind Reader

With Dyson, let's look at the main, or primary, associations in each of the three countries. The scale down the side indicates the percentage of people who had a particular impression of the brand or product.

The first thing to note is the sheer quantity of associations and impressions. For example, in the UK, over 50 percent of people mention the key product feature of no bags, and then, at 33 percent and 30 percent, the performance and power of the machine.

In Germany, baglessness is even more important. Half of people mention no bags, and then another 23 percent talk about no Hoover bags. And Germans, being more engineering-literate that their Anglo-American cousins, can tell us what this feature means: "no loss of suction" (31 percent) and "100 percent suction" (18 percent). But note the colour profile compared with the UK: the lighter shading tells us that their views are less tempered. The enthusiasm is less deep-rooted, as befits a country with lower ownership of the product.

The only negative primary impression, in all countries, is price. This is an expensive piece of kit. And in the US, that's the strongest impression. We'll see why this is in a moment.

Everywhere, there's relatively little doubt about what's going on. This works—and works differently. It stands out as a piece of design. It costs. Frankly, it's a salesman's wet dream.

Top associations with Dyson

UK
100 respondents

Germany
101 respondents

US
101 respondents

% UK		% Germany		% US	
50	Bagless	50	Bagless	61	Expensive
35	Expensive	31	No loss of suction	41	Great suction
33	Great performance	23	No Hoover bags	38	Bagless
30	Powerful	22	Vacuum cleaner	27	Designed differently
26	Well-designed	21	Good design	22	Better than other vacuums
24	Colourful	20	Television advertising	20	Well-made
24	Good at cleaning	18	Expensive	17	Doesn't clog
20	Efficient	18	Top product	14	Spins dirt out of air
17	Quality	18	Expensive but good	9	Dude's [Dyson's] accent
15	Innovative	18	100% suction	9	Good vacuum

A more convenient way of getting rid of dust: Germany

Let's look at Germany first, since they seem to know what's going on.

Dyson first entered the German market in 1998 and currently has a 6.8 percent share. The competitive conditions are as onerous as anywhere else.

Half of Germans mention no bags. But their main interpretation is that this means a saving in expensive bags and a more convenient way of getting rid of dust. One third "get" no loss of suction: the idea that there is a better way of separating the dust from the air so that there is no clogging up of the machine. The striking design also figures strongly in their impressions: "it doesn't look like any others, it must be special"; "the perfect form, the perfect function."

And we get the sort of comment that continues to cause the Dyson marketer to applaud and simultaneously tear out their hair. The sort of comment that comes from someone who nearly gets it, but not quite. Mr Dyson had problems with hoovering, so he invented the Hoover with no loss of suction.

Well they ain't cheap, not at four or five hundred bucks: US

The primary, and largely negative association in the US is with price. The first thing Americans are likely to think is that this is expensive. Let's put this in context, however. Dyson is a premium product. Many people do see it as beyond their means, and to some, it genuinely is. To others, it just doesn't make sense to shell out that kind of money on a vacuum cleaner.

Dyson associations, US

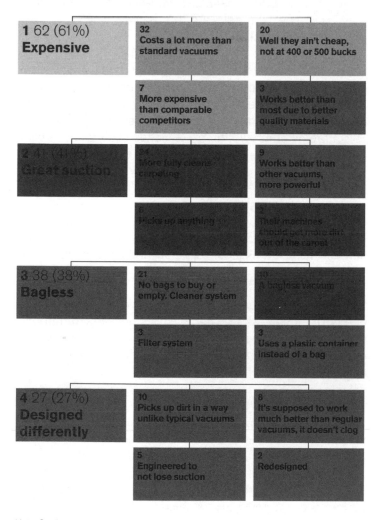

1 62 (61%) **Expensive**	**32** Costs a lot more than standard vacuums	**20** Well they ain't cheap, not at 400 or 500 bucks
	7 More expensive than comparable competitors	**3** Works better than most due to better quality materials
2 41 (41%) **Great suction**	**24** More fully cleans carpeting	**9** Works better than other vacuums, more powerful
	6 Picks up anything	**2** Their machines should get more dirt out of the carpet
3 38 (38%) **Bagless**	**21** No bags to buy or empty. Cleaner system	**10** A bagless vacuum
	3 Filter system	**3** Uses a plastic container instead of a bag
4 27 (27%) **Designed differently**	**10** Picks up dirt in a way unlike typical vacuums	**8** It's supposed to work much better than regular vacuums, it doesn't clog
	5 Engineered to not lose suction	**2** Redesigned

Note: Single comments/mentions are excluded in this chart.

Of course, to any half decent salesman, the objection that your product is expensive is manna from heaven. "You're absolutely right," they say, "and here are the reasons why." And then you're in a conversation.

In the UK, Stella Artois (now available on deal in any local supermarket) spent millions of pounds and years on a campaign called "Reassuringly Expensive," in which it made pains to emphasize how teasingly inaccessible this beer was. This strategy does two things. It makes plain to those who can afford it that this is something worth trying. And to those who can't, it sets up a background whisper that one day they might be able to.

Dyson doesn't go out of its way to stress the expense of the product. But one suspects that it doesn't fret about this perception. It creates a conversation, and begs the question, "Why?"

Otherwise, the US gets it. Kind of. It's got great suction (41 percent); it's bagless (38 percent); it's designed differently (27 percent). But look into the secondary associations with each of these and you see that very few people know, or can explain why, this technology is better.

The mother ship: UK
The UK is Dyson's most mature market: it currently has a 39 percent share. One in three households has a Dyson. So this is what a seasoned bunch of people think about the cleaner. Their headlines are: it's bagless and it's expensive. Underneath this, there is lots of praise for the functional performance: great performance; it's powerful; it's efficient. There is also plenty of praise for the aesthetics: well-designed and colourful.

Dyson associations, UK

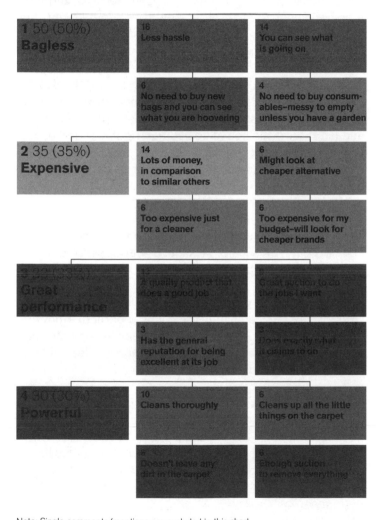

1 50 (50%) Bagless	16 Less hassle	14 You can see what is going on
	6 No need to buy new bags and you can see what you are hoovering	4 No need to buy consumables–messy to empty unless you have a garden
2 35 (35%) Expensive	14 Lots of money, in comparison to similar others	6 Might look at cheaper alternative
	6 Too expensive just for a cleaner	6 Too expensive for my budget–will look for cheaper brands
3 30 (30%) Great performance	17 A quality product that does a good job	8 Great suction to do the jobs I want
	3 Has the general reputation for being excellent at its job	3 Does exactly what it claims to do
4 30 (30%) Powerful	10 Cleans thoroughly	6 Cleans up all the little things on the carpet
	8 Doesn't leave any dirt in the carpet	6 Enough suction to remove everything

Note: Single comments/mentions are excluded in this chart.

Now this is a pretty good list. Remember, we're not asking for what people think is good about Dyson: we're asking them for what comes to mind when they think about Dyson, then following that path. People come up with a number of good qualities at respectable levels.

What is interesting is that the principal feature "bagless" is misunderstood. Or, let's say, not fully understood. The point about being bagless is that it allows the separation of dust and air at fantastic speed so you don't get clogged up and you don't lose suction. What people talk about is that it saves you money on bags and makes it a bit easier to get rid of the dust.

Very rarely, at least in the UK, do people talk about why the Dyson is better, other than the generic value of sucking well. They are buying a superb package: powerful, sleek and good looking. What else they are buying we'll look at in Chapter 3.

Mostly, we don't get it

Dyson's key technical innovation was a particular physical feature—the cyclonic construction. This feature separates dust and air effectively by removing the clogging effect of bags, thereby maintaining a high level of suction.

As the data shows, apart from a minority in emerging markets, no-one really gets this. You sense this is a real source of frustration for some of the people at Dyson. They talk wistfully about how clued up Japanese housewives will describe the technological advantages in detail.

"The marketing job here is that you've got something much better but it's bloody complicated to tell people [about] . . ."[4]
Clare Mullin, Dyson Group Marketing Director

We have to remember that Dyson people are believers. They have inherited the mantle of rational progress: that we can engineer and have a better world. It's not enough for you to think your Dyson is pretty good at getting up the dust. They want you to know why.

The evidence is that most people don't, even in the UK market, where Dyson has now been established for over ten years. What they know is that Dysons work pretty well and look pretty good. For most companies this would be fine. Car makers, for example, have engines and chassis stuffed full of fascinating innovations, but they've long since given up trying to explain how they work. The strategy is to create a product, imbue it with a certain identity and then stud it with lots of functional credentials.

But that doesn't cut it with Dyson people. It's important to them that we know how and why cyclones work; and, for that matter, multiple cyclones, HEPA filters and beater brushes. It's important because, unlike most other manufacturing businesses, Dyson is a business where

the engineers are still in charge.

Had things taken a different, more conventional path, and the Dyson product been bought or franchised by another business, and we'd been flies on the wall in a conference room, we would have heard something like this:

Marketing chief

I think the research is pretty conclusive. We may be wasting a lot of time and energy trying to get over the details of quite why this works. Consumers haven't got the attention span.

James Dyson

Yes, but it's fundamental to this product that people understand why it's better by understanding how it works. Why else would they pay more?

Marketing chief

James, James. When you fly, you don't wonder how the plane works; when you use your laptop, you don't try to figure out how it's doing all that clever stuff.

James Dyson

Yes I do.

Marketing chief

Well ... I don't. In fact, I'm sure most normal people don't. Why don't we look at some the campaigns that have been worked up. Dyson: Simply Better. This works for me ... Jeff?

Sales chief

And by simplifying the message right down, we'll be able to train shop floor people that much more quickly.

Marketing chief
> And consumers won't get so confused so they won't phone the call centre as much. Probably. Everyone wins.

We're now beginning to locate the main source of energy of the Dyson company and idea. It's about the engineering, stupid. They are in ideological conflict with convention at two levels:

1   The vacuum cleaner/home appliance industry, which they regard as made up of a bunch of lazy hawkers who couldn't design their way out of a paper bag.

2   Our cultural failure to embrace the possibility of rational progress by applying skill and ingenuity to our problems. Things could be better if we thought more clearly, acted more restlessly and invested more appropriately. And were generally a lot less satisfied with what passes for adequate in our society.

Frequently, the stimulus for innovation is this profound dissatisfaction with what exists. Another suction entrepreneur is Mandy Haberman, inventor of the Haberman Feeder (and subsequently the Anywayup Cup), a milk bottle that allows children with facial or oral problems to feed more easily than with a conventional bottle. The invention originated when Haberman's own daughter Emily was born with a condition that made it difficult for her to suck. Haberman became so frustrated with trying to find a way to feed her baby that she was driven to invention.

"The driving force wasn't to create a successful product or to make money . . . Something needed to be done and no-one else was doing anything about it. The energy came from anger. I didn't see why other people should have to go through what I went through trying to feed my daughter." [5]

A little like James Dyson's experience with the "poxy machine" we saw in Chapter 1.

Mandy Haberman probably wouldn't describe herself as an engineer, but the engineering mentality is clearly in charge.

Engineers often distrust or demean marketing because they believe it departs from the purity of their solution. One Microsoft employee told me about his engineers:

"What you're dealing with is people who genuinely believe that if you could just get customers to read the spec sheet, they'd flock to the product."

It's important to an engineer not just that you understand that something works better, but that you understand why. From their point of view, how could you just accept it without a clear rational underpinning?

"A lot of what we do is very tedious . . . but the more you get into it you realize how fascinating it is. Endless test results . . . the difference between what works and

**what doesn't . . . that give us our know-
how, our patents, our technology. For all
of us doing it, that's what we like doing—
coming in every day, being disappointed,
spending your day scratching your
head and solving problems and building
prototypes."** [6]
Interview with James Dyson, 2005

The vast majority of life as an engineer is devoted to getting
things wrong. Or rather, to painstakingly testing things to see
how they might work. Thomas Edison famously said that
he discovered more than 2,000 ways of how not to make
a light bulb, blowing up several labs along the way. And
this process is going on as you read, in thousands of
workshops, pharmaceutical labs and software businesses
worldwide. Having got so much wrong, an engineer–designer
wants you to be clear about why they've got it right. This
is a generous impulse. They don't want you to go through the
pain they did.

Dyson resist calling themselves a brand, because that seems to
them flippant and hucksterish. They are representatives of an
ideology. This is the engineer's ideology: what's important is that
you can make stuff better.

The words engine and engineer come from the Latin adjective
ingeniosus, meaning "skilled." An engineer is thus a skilled,
practical, problem solver. One of the features of modern day
culture is that we no longer hold these engineering skills
in the esteem they once enjoyed. In the 1950s in Britain
(when James Dyson was being brought up), the virtues of the

great Victorian engineers—Telford, Stephenson, Brunel—were trumpeted in the school syllabus.

Indeed, as this book was being finalized, Dyson announced plans to build his own school of design and engineering in Bath.

One thing you notice when you talk to engineers, including those from Dyson, is that they are pragmatists as well as idealists. They want to make things better so they search for things that will work; this is Utopianism with its feet on the ground. Driven by the idea that most things are possible, they embark on lengthy experiments and grand schemes. They then spend weeks or years discarding things. Because it either works, or it doesn't. The climax of this is the moment when it actually works. This moment might be the plastic seal on the bottom of a vacuum cleaner that no-one will ever see or it might be the maiden flight of a passenger jet. It's when the astronauts splash down, mission completed. It's the moment that no-one can ever take away from you.

Culturally, engineers are characterized by, and often parodied for the quality of intensity they bring to problem solving and life generally. (Dilbert's an engineer.) Engineering has two principal values. The first is that it means things get built and done. Roads are constructed, software programmes designed, printing presses built. The second is that it reinforces the potent beliefs.

We're about to plunge into the philosophical pool, but don't worry, we'll be out and towelling ourselves down soon. As human beings we can only be certain of two things: that we're going to die; that we don't know when. These facts lurk around our everyday lives, and most of us do our level best to ignore them, or drown out their promptings. One of the ways we deal with them is to construct sets of beliefs that help us make sense of them. One of the most potent is the idea of progress: that we can take command of our surroundings by the use of science and technology.

We would like to believe in a better future. The Dyson is a symbol of this belief. By buying a Dyson, we reinvest in this belief. Like all consumer goods, it offers temporary respite from the problems that life offers up: in this case, the sense that our home (and thereby we) are less clean than we'd like to think we are.

Technology brands such as Microsoft, Apple or Vodafone rely absolutely on the virtues of progress. They offer, packaged ever more expertly and sexily, more potent versions of your future. As brands, they have arrogated the esteem that used to be attributed to the inventors and engineers.

"Believers in progress are seeking from technology what they once looked for in political ideologies and before in religion—salvation from themselves." [7]
John Gray, professor at the London School of Economics

Jeffre Jackson, former planning director at Weiden & Kennedy, puts it like this: "One of the functions of a brand is that people find it a useful way of thinking about things. And Dyson—if you think about it—is a very useful idea: you can make the world better by pure engineering." [8]

One of the attractions of the idea of progress is its fundamental optimism. Far from being playthings of the universe, we can assert some control. In the objects we create, we can literally take hold of it. And we can do so with a smile on our face. The joy of acquiring a well-designed new phone, handbag or pair of shoes is the joy of temporarily asserting our own hopes and beliefs in ourselves, in the future.

Of course, as every respectable sci-fi novel or film will tell you, we'll still have intractable human issues to deal with. But we'll deal with them more hopefully.

All this may seem a far cry from vacuum cleaners. But I hope you'll see why it's important. When you buy a Dyson, you aren't just buying a very good vacuum cleaner. You're voting for the idea that somewhere the engineers are still in charge. They've got something that works better. Even if you don't quite understand what they're going on about when they explain it.

Chapter 3
The Good Life: Sanctuary and Domestic Weaponry

"They're into all that now they've got the extension. They've got one of those silver bins ... and a Dyson."

Overheard on the No. 65 bus in Brentford

Without stressing you, let's think, for a moment, about stress. In 2000, the Trades Union Congress surveyed 9,000 health and safety representatives across all industrial sectors in the UK. It was trying to understand the main workplace hazards facing workers and managers. Stress came out as top in most of the industries: 86 percent of those in the banking and finance industries, 74 percent in the health service. [9]

Over the past century, individuals like you and me have become shock absorbers in a way our minds weren't designed for. We live in transitional societies, where the protean nature of our lives is evident and even celebrated. The taken-for-granted structures of family, organization and geography increasingly no longer apply. What was called society is disaggregating, as more young people live alone, more old people live alone, and the ones in the middle divorce with increasing frequency. These same people are less and less likely to be employed by a large organization, or any organization and, where they are, that employment is more contingent than ever before. Job mobility is required, nationally and internationally, and with it, the sense of belonging to a particular town or region recedes.

Stress has become part of our everyday discourse. We use the word in a way our forebears, even 20 years ago, would never have done. How are you? Oh, a bit stressed. He's de-stressing next door. She's all stressed up. Don't get so stressed about it.

Being inventive creatures, humans seek remedies for this chronic stress. Church going increases, as does self-exploration, whether through therapy or the Internet. Technology promises us control of the chaos (your entire CD collection on one small

MP3 player!). Holidays and travelling become more exotic and less packaged.

What characterizes many of these responses is the claim of psychological self-determination and, within it, the sense of turning in on oneself. Part of this process is looking in towards our own homes, something that Shoshana Zuboff and James Maxmin have described as a claim on "sanctuary".[10]

The claim on sanctuary is expressed in many ways. It has broadly three aspects:

— Designing the space

— Cleansing the space

— Possessing the space

Designing the space

I'm sitting having tea with Mickey, who's been a building contractor in West London for 15 years. Business is booming They're all trapped round here, he says. "They can't afford to buy another house so they've got to build space into what they've got: an extra bedroom here or a kitchen extension there. Everyone wants the good life, see."[11]

"The good life" is his code for the redesign and reallocation of space that preoccupies increasing numbers of those people seeking sanctuary. The more we feel old certainties about ourselves and our place in the world ebb away, the more important the quality of our own space, and our ability to author or control that space, becomes. In the UK, this has gone beyond the do-it-yourself boom of the 1980s and 90s, although that market is still worth in excess of £9bn per year. The culture of home improvement is all-pervasive. Magazines, websites and broadcast television are all testimony to this hunger, as well as inciting it.

As more and more people turn from the world, the home must accommodate more of the features that the world used to provide. We bring work home, or we work from home, so spare rooms become offices. Dedicated exercise spaces are created. Home theatre attempts to bring the theatre home. Within a household, people need or count on their own space. We now routinely assume that a child will want their own room. In 1970, the average house in the US had one and a half bathrooms; by 1997, it was two and a half.

Our desire for different and more flexible space is guided by another set of assumptions about how the space should look. Semioticians, those experts in unpacking the symbolism of objects and media, tend to classify phenomena into one of three areas in a given subject area: the historic, the dominant and the emergent. Things are organized in the same way as art galleries. The national gallery shows you what's happened; the modern art building shows you what's just past its peak; the contemporary art gallery shows all the experiments, some of which may have potential. Commercial semioticians are particularly interested in the emergent, because it gives them clues to where the mainstream is heading, and that's where the big money is. Below is an example of mainstream domestic space tastes.

Historic Pre 1990s	Dominant 1990s–Present	Emergent Current experiments
Controlled space: separate rooms with specific functions (dining, drawing)	Flexible/merging space: home offices, open kitchen/dining areas	Deliberately designed home/work apartments
Strong use of colour	Cleanness and lightness of lines	Rebellion against clean lines and miminalism
	More restrained uses of colour	Use of industrial motifs
	Search for country/authentic reference points and natural materials	

These big movements in taste have implications for all the businesses that supply the home. Beech floor traders, lighting suppliers and purveyors of flagstones and granite have all done well in the last ten years. The lightening and de-cluttering of homes puts more of your space on view, so part of the task is to find ways of keeping that space looking like it should.

Cleansing the space

This renewed attention on the home requires the space to be safe. This means security at the physical or "structural" level—as I leaf through home improvement blogs, I see plenty of advertising for burglar alarms and security systems. And it means security at the level of cleanliness.

Let's go down to the world of dirt. It broadly works at three levels, says a source in the home-cleaning business. The first is at the obvious physical level: dirt, stains and dust that you can see and that demand removal because they're soiling your view. The second is at the bacterial level: the germs that invite destruction because of their evil properties. They infect you and cause damage to you and your family. The third is at the molecular level: the allergens and pollutants that you routinely ingest through your breath or skin—the ones that remain mysterious. They can't be destroyed, but they can be displaced or removed.

Psychologically, dirt symbolizes disorder, which is the very thing causing stress in the external world. The mind seeks ways of bolstering itself against this anxiety: creating security and order in our surroundings is part of our medicine. These impulses are universal. We need to feel good about where we live. But what we've seen in the past few years in the West has been an abundance of products and services to help the middle classes reinforce a sense of psychological security in the home environment. The design of kitchens and kitchen appliances is increasingly sleek and metallic. Cleaning ladies are everywhere. Cleaning products have become condensed into gels and powerballs. These products have trigger sprays, and delightfully combative names like Cillit Bang. More watts, more rpm, more effectiveness. Product and graphic design emphasizes their power, and they become armoured by language, too.

Lock nozzle flip into arrow on the top before use.
Instructions for a surface to air missile?
No, just those for our kitchen cleaning spray.

Possessing the space
Let's listen in on some depth interviews I conducted a couple of years back into domesticity and the domestic sphere:

> **"It's like, it's my space [indicated kitchen/living area] and my environment . . . and I'm in command round here!"**

> **"What I want to do is get the place sorted quite quickly when I get in from work, so it's all quite intense for 15 minutes or so till it's back like it should be in my mind."**

> **"Look at that [entering the front door after the cleaner had been] . . . she's been. It's all perfect again."**

Three different women with different needs from the environment. To the first, this was her territory and you didn't mess. The second had a requirement for speed and potency in restoring the environment to her mental ideal. The third delegated the task of remedying the disorder to someone else. In each case, they were restoring the worth and security of their environment. To do this effectively, you need tools for the job.

Enter the Dyson

> **"Any kind of possession really functions as an extension of our own personal power."**
> Ernest Dichter, *The Strategy of Desire*

What we're tracing is the intersection of three phenomena. The increasing attention paid to the home space and its maintenance is one. We then see the traditional aversion to dust, dirt and bacteria that drives much household cleaning, with emerging concerns about allergens, asthma and skin complaints. And finally we see the products, graphics and language that emphasize the power and potency of the user. Enter the Dyson.

An early press ad for the brand shows a fairly revolting pile of dust and fluff. It's labelled dust mite faeces, viruses, pollen, pet hairs. The proposition is that bags lose suction, leaving this lot in your home. The simple provocation of disgust, plus the promise of immediate and continuing annihilation. It's a heady cocktail.

One of my interviewees grabs the telescopic handle, points it at no-one in particular and utters the immortal words of Sigourney Weaver in *Alien*: "Get back, bitch!"

Alan Fletcher, the sadly departed eminence grise of graphic design and author of *The Art of Looking Sideways* stares

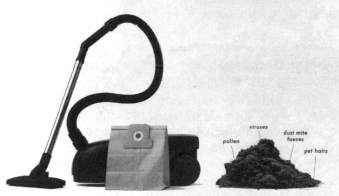

Bags kill suction, leaving this in your home.

The Dyson has no bag and no loss of suction.

Now you can see what gets left behind when your vacuum cleaner stops sucking properly. Ordinary vacuum cleaners work by sucking air through a bag. But as soon as dust goes into the bag, it starts to clog. After just one room, suction can be down as much as 50%. And the more you use it, the worse it gets. Only one cleaner has solved this problem - the Dyson. With its Dual Cyclone technology and no bag, it gives 100% suction, 100% of the time. For further information, call Dyson on 0870 60 70 888. **www.dyson.com** **dyson** at the same gunmetal DC08 and says, "It looks like a pet robot, but from the Navy."

Comments a friend on buying his first Dyson: "It looked like it was going to do the business, unlike those beige and grey objects of your childhood."

Part of the brilliance of Dyson was to enter the market and break the rules of the category when they badly needed to broken. Even in the early 1990s, most vacuum cleaners looked like they were just emerging from the 1970s. Metaphorically, they had sideburns. They doddered around like extras in an early police drama, wheezing and ineffective. This was the stage on which the first Dyson upright, the DC01, entered. Twelve years on, it might strike some of you as a little ungainly. But then it was nothing short of a revolution.

The machine looked uncompromising. It was a systematic assault on the conventional wisdom of the market at the time.

One of the rules was that because the majority of vacuuming is done by women, vacuums should be feminized, cushioned, discreet; the dirt and workings concealed from a female eye. "I won't be a moment," they should say, "then you can put me back in the cupboard."

The DC01, by contrast, was unapologetically a machine. Dyson talked about achieving that "NASA look." The design showcases the machinery, rather as the contemporaneous Lloyd's building in London used open space architecture and transparency to open the world to its workings.

The DC01

Dyson had spent years making the cyclone work and he wanted you to see it spinning and where the dirt went, to help you understand what was going on. "Look!" it screams. "No bag!" This was Dyson's Brunelian moment. A Brunel suspension bridge shows a curve not because it is easy on the eye, but because it follows the mathematics of nature; the design of the DC01 followed the engineering.

The other kidney punch to convention was the insight that if you confront people with their dirt, they will acknowledge the power of the machine that has removed it, rather than simply balk in disgust.

Over the long haul, the greatest coup of the transparent bin has been the way it alerts, warns, amazes or puts to shame the person who is watching how it fills up. This turns into conversation.

> **"I'm looking at this, and I'm thinking, this is all my shit, and there's loads of it."**
>
> **"God, I know, there was three buckets of the stuff."** [12]
> Two Dyson users talking

Thousands of these conversations have created the expectation that your Dyson will spin dirt out of the carpet or flooring in front of your eyes. And, lo and behold, it does.

Think of the store impact. There was a bunch of grey and blue vacuums and then a big, brassy silver and yellow thing with a transparent bin full of rubbish. You may not have liked it but you couldn't ignore it.

Striking colourways had already been part of Dyson's signature. The pink and lavender of the G-Force were forerunners of the entry colours of silver and yellow, and the purples and limes that we see today.

Finally, there was the sturdy build of the body. There was a sense of purpose about the construction: it dispensed with the complications of height adjustment, vertical release pedals and coil reflex units. Tools such as brushes and nozzles were designed to integrate by fitting on to the body of the machine. It meant business.

Twelve years on, we're staring at one of the latest models—the cylinder DC08, the one described by Alan Fletcher as a naval pet robot. It's all coiled power and purpose. Integration has moved on so that you can now wrap the hose around the machine and secure it. It sits there, squat, just so. Transparency still dominates. Technology has moved on so I now have eight little cyclones doing my work for me. They sit atop the main body, a shell-like array of bunched muscles.

I unwrap the hose from the body, take hold of the sculpted handle of the main cleaning part, click a button with my thumb and the telescopic extension unfolds. Somewhere in the back of my mind a US marine shouts, "You will strip and clean this in 60 seconds or you're out of this unit." My accessories are clipped snugly to the hose. Get back, bitch.

One of my early interviewees, a lady, said, "The thing about a Dyson is, you see, that it makes it personal." I know what she means.

It's the machine that strode into the domestic arena. It's stylish muscle.

The status of the task

"Every status has its symbol"
Lufthansa slogan

The good life's requirement for cleansed space is evident. The next task is how to make the act of cleansing satisfying and rewarding.

We have to be careful here. Any hard-boiled Dyson engineer would blanch at the suggestion that their product was a status symbol. It's just a great piece of engineering, they'd say. And they'd be right. But being humans, we use it, inescapably, as a status symbol.

Examine the brands that have come to populate the middle class home—Habitat (UK), Crate & Barrel (US), Ikea (everywhere). They ask us to look anew at our everyday environments and possessions: their ambition is that we sequentially upgrade pretty much everything. As well as making money out of the serious upgrades of kitchens, redecorating or crockery, they make a great deal of cash on the replacement mugs, utensils, towels, chairs or paint that we use and see every day. They promise a little more satisfaction and reward in the ordinary. This joy tends to be short-lived and elusive, but that's another story.

When we buy our scented candles, our beech dining tables or our stainless steel chef's hob, we buy conferred status. Or, depending on how severe you want to be, we buy participation in our fantasies of what our life could be. We buy a dark, well-gripped potato peeler, and with it the expertise of peeling like a pro. We buy the simple white crockery, and with it the confidence of the relaxed host. We buy the black and white prints and with them the security of the discreet. My personal *bête noire* is the Aga, a massively expensive range cooker that is bought for one reason only: to engage in the fantasy of the country kitchen where privately educated children rush in from the garden to be served a casserole that Mother has knocked together while organizing the village fête, while Father is doing something distant and Professional.

Status, disentangled from its pejorative sense, has two dimensions. It is Janus-faced. Inwardly, your purchase satisfies your own want, or lack, maintaining your story about yourself. Outwardly, it is part of how you inform others about you. This is obvious in the purchase of say, breast enhancement or sports cars, but less so in the domestic arena.

It becomes clear when we understand how we use symbols to demonstrate our preferences and enthusiasms: a flag, a perfume, a home. These symbols give us a sense of personal value, completion or power, and, crucially, demonstrate this to others. This is only rarely in a "showy" sense, or as a demonstration of one-upmanship. We have to demonstrate or signal status to others because as social beings we need continual feedback from others in order to maintain our sense of ourselves. Objects, in this sense, are a form of conversation between ourselves and the world. That's why, in traditional story telling, the protagonist lays claim to an object (a sword, amulet, glass slipper) that represents the qualities the story celebrates. By possessing the object, you possess the quality the object represents. In the case of food, drink or beauty products, you literally incorporate (take into your body) the features of the product.

Given this, what form of status does Dyson confer? What conversations is it prompting?

First and foremost, it confers capability. As we have seen, Dyson introduced a new form of weaponry into the domestic arsenal. But more subtly, we acquire the sense of performance: we are working at a more effective and more satisfying rate. We are being offered a more rewarding experience of keeping order. We are a Good Householder, even if we only spend ten minutes a day in this role.

As one Dyson owner told me "You just get this sense that it's doing a good job . . . and that you're doing a good job."

Outwardly, Dysons confer status in two ways. First, they make few concessions to the traditional assumptions of what vacuum cleaners look like. They say, "I have made a different choice from the mainstream." They invite conversation, and they get it. I don't have the numbers, but I would wager that Dysons spend proportionately longer out of the cupboard and on display than their competitors. The organization will gently discourage any sense that the machine is there to be admired, rather than to be used. But in the next sentence they will enthuse about how many design museums have it on display. On every machine, a little leaflet proclaims:

"Dyson products are on display at the following museums: Science Museum, Victoria and Albert Museum in London; Boymans Museum in Rotterdam; San Francisco Museum of Modern Art; Museum fur Angewandte Kunst in Cologne; Zurich Design Museum; Georges Pompidou

**Centre in Paris; Design Museum
in Lisbon and Powerhouse Museum
in Sydney, to name a few."**

The design principles are all about showcasing the engineering and emphasizing the functionality. But in practice, the conversation in households in Japan (where the prototype G-Force sold at upwards of $2,000) and the UK was roughly:

"It looks weird/alien/cool."

"It's pink."

"You can see the dirt inside."

The first two allow the owner, however briefly, to bask in the glow of reflected discernment, imagining that the other party is thinking, "I'd never have dared or risked this." The owner is running a tighter ship, with more interesting toys. There is a market for vacuum cleaners. It intersects with the market for helping us feel more competent than our peers. "Dyson really revolutionized the entire market," says Nick Platt, a vacuum cleaner expert at retail audit group GfK.

**"They changed the nature of the product
into an aesthetic lifestyle product, a status
symbol."** [13]
BBC online

The final comment is the important one, since it allows the owner to justify an expensive purchase in purely rational terms. "Well, just look at what it's got up. You would not believe it. I was a bit embarrassed/astonished." This conversation engages the non-owner in a series of anxiety provoking reflections about the cleanliness of their own homes, involving a diminution of their own status.

What was required was a product that rewarded a joyless, everyday task, while simultaneously conferring status. And that's what the world got. How it got it is the subject of the next chapter.

Chapter 4
The Adventure

"To invent,
you need
a good
imagination
and a
pile of junk."

Thomas Edison

"I must have felt that life was trundling along far too easily and that it was time to chuck something hefty in its way, an exhausting instinct whose constant reiterations in my life I have been suffering from ever since." [14]
James Dyson on starting to play the bassoon, the most difficult instrument in the orchestra

I'm holding *Against the Odds*, James Dyson's autobiography. It's a very good read. A man alone, striving for what he feels is right, puts at risk his own health and his family's security, in order to defeat the forces of ignorance and corporate chicanery. He emerges into the light, laying claim to fame, fortune and the justice of his convictions.

The animating force of the story is the right to justice: that you should be recompensed, not damaged, for being true to yourself and your views. In one sense, the story is only co-incidentally about vacuum cleaners. It is about life force—the possibility that through our own efforts, we can become more complete.

He has a well developed and, possibly, well justified persecution complex.

"This is ultimately about how I took on the big boys at their own game and made them look very silly, just by being true to myself." [15]

This is both the truth and necessary myth of James Dyson and the company that bears his name.

Nothing but the virtues of a mule
At the beginning of the first chapter, there is an astonishing, deeply poignant form of preface.

> **"Misfits are not born or made; they make themselves. A stubborn, opinionated child, desperate to be different and to be right, encounters only smaller refractions of the problems he will always experience. And he carries the weight of that dislocation for ever."** [16]

Dyson had a feeling of difference from a very young age, careering around the big Victorian house attached to Gresham's School in Norfolk, where his father was a classics teacher. He was the youngest of three children. The seminal event of his childhood is his father's death, when the young James was aged nine. He records how that affected him, breeding a sense of ultra-competitiveness and of not being thwarted in his ambition as his father—who had been about to change career to join the BBC—had been. Later, he recalls "the ignominy of second-rate academic performance, few friends and no dad."

He discovered long-distance running as an outlet for his nervous energy, enjoying the absolute clarity of performance against time or against others, the sense of visible results as he improved, and, above all, the qualities of stamina and obstinacy that were to serve him so well.

Intriguingly, another great company has, as part of its founding myth, long-distance running. Nike started as a shoe business, with an obsession about improving the performance of athletes, celebrated in a famous press ad, in which your view is from the inside of a crowded restaurant and you see, at the window, the blur of a passing runner. "You've either run today, or you haven't," says the line.

Regarded as a failure by his school, but showing a talent for painting, Dyson moved to London in 1966 to attend art school, where he met his wife and won a scholarship to the Royal College of Art, a centre of excellence in the emerging disciplines of interior, furniture and product design. He encountered the structural engineer Anthony Hunt, the designer of Waterloo Station and became fascinated both by structure and its aesthetics. Even then, Dyson's imagination was populated by the achievements of the male heroes that are a feature of his autobiography and, we assume, his internal narrative. Isambard Kingdom Brunel and Buckminster Fuller feature at this early stage. Indeed, he claims that Brunel's story, "enabled me to see my career as a whole and to know that it would turn out the way it has."

Heroes were necessary bulwarks against a raging "fear of failure, one which drove me on then and still does." Through his first encounter with big business, a meeting with Vickers where they laughed him off, Dyson was put in touch with a crucial figure—both a hero and a practical mentor, Jeremy Fry. (There was a poignancy to my research in November 2005, as Fry's funeral was taking place.) A pivotal moment in the Dyson narrative occurs when he meets Fry, the managing director of Rotork, and has a form of practical epiphany: that you can talk about ideas and design, build wonderful things and make millions of pounds.

Dyson joined Rotork and embarked on a project called the Sea Truck, a quasi-military large-scale speedboat with a construction that allowed it to move faster through water. What's intriguing about this stage of Dyson's life is that he is not brought on by Fry as an apprentice designer, but as the director of the marine division of a public company, with full responsibility for innovation, delivery and sales. At 24, and with nothing but a degree from art college to cover his modesty, he does a deal with the Egyptian military to provide half a dozen stripped down boats which a month later land at the Sinai to destroy Israeli defence positions. The Libyans are next, and a cash-wielding Swiss gangster. Critical here are his developing skills as a salesman, and not a salesman of anything, but of something he invented himself. Dyson's control needs were high, and the combination of being the inventor, chief propagandist and quality control chief served these needs well.

1974–78

Coincidence or providence? That depends on your point of view. But life moves us in important tangents, and so it was with James Dyson. An abortive attempt to develop increased protection for the hull of the Sea Truck, led to an understanding of how to mould polythene into a sphere. Simultaneously, a move to a farmhouse in Gloucestershire, and the financial requirement to do a lot of rebuilding work himself, led Dyson to spend a lot of time with wheelbarrows. In an eerie anticipation of his later work with the vacuum cleaner, we see a trance-like involvement with an overlooked domestic object, as, driven by personal frustration and sheer curiosity, he sets to changing the form of the offending item. The wheelbarrow he uses is unstable with heavy loads. It digs ruts in the lawn. It has thin strut-like legs that sink into soft ground. Its sharp steel edges damage your legs and your doors.

The Ballbarrow

The result, eventually, was the Ballbarrow, featuring a moulded ball instead of the wheel, and a more rounded, balanced body, with fatter feet.

These are classic tales of creation, when need and chance observation coincide. Classically, Gutenberg noticed that the combined actions of a coin punch and of a wine press could form the basis of the printing press.

Emboldened, Dyson handed in his notice at Rotork. His wife Deirdre, who strikes you as an extraordinarily supportive partner, encourages this venture. He forms Kirk-Dyson, holding 50 percent of the business alongside his brother-in-law. There is another brush with a short-sighted industrial giant, ICI. (We will see how these companies become, for Dyson, symbols for all that is indolent and oppressive about modern business.)

We get a glimpse of how he uses colour in signalling difference to potential buyers. In applying for Design Council endorsement of his design, he receives feedback that the ball, then red, should be green like the body of the barrow, the better to complement a garden. Piqued, Dyson then makes the ball as luridly orange as possible. We notice how he derives energy from being knocked back, when so many others might quail. The marketing of the product is both wayward and maverick. The breakthrough is to sell direct to the public, rather than through the recalcitrant building and gardening trade. A key lesson is making journalists fans of the product so the good news spreads—a fundamental feature of Dyson marketing that persists today. Within a year or two, the product has 50 percent of the wheelbarrow market, and is at a 200–300 percent premium to the regular barrow.

Kirk-Dyson nevertheless struggles under the weight of debt it accrued at start-up and through investment in new production. Dyson's shareholding is diluted and with it his voice and influence. It is to this he largely attributes the decline of the business, which was accompanied by a series of misadventures in the attempt to license the Ballbarrow in the US.

Fuelled, as we have seen, by knockbacks, Dyson now experiences successive and visceral senses of betrayal—from a venal sales manager, a copycat US manufacturer and, finally, the board of Kirk-Dyson, which ousts him unceremoniously. He rationalizes the actions of his colleagues as jealous antipathy towards the main man's profile and creativity. But there is genuine loss here. He loses his invention (for the patent was assigned to the company) and the relationship with his sister, a co-investor, is fractured.

A year earlier, Dyson had lost his mother to cancer. We do not know the effect this had—but we can speculate. Many people's response to the death of their remaining parent is intense grief and a sense of being lost in the world, but equally, an emergent sense of relief. A colleague in his fifties, successful in any sense of the word, describes this: "It's uncanny, but I have this sense now that I'm not doing things for anyone else, to anyone else's expectations. I'm able, almost for the first time, to do what I want to do."

Alone, as he records, but a little wiser, Dyson was learning not just that things had to be on his terms—he'd always really known that anyway—but what those terms should be. His way, or the highway.

1978: This poxy machine

At a new property, but yoked by the familiar heavy mortgage and a need to do his own remodelling, we find Dyson, in the final stages of his relationship with Kirk-Dyson, disconsolately vacuuming his way around his house.

(Mythically, the home is the place where the adventurer comes to lick his wounds, to farm, to think, to prepare for the next adventure. This is where the hero really wants to be, but is compelled to right wrongs in the external world.)

As with the Ballbarrrow, we encounter the heady mix of a need, observation and a profoundly curious mind. This need is borne of the engineer's frustration with substandard equipment, in this case a vacuum cleaner that gradually declines in its performance.

Imagine if the standard bicycle behaved like this. On every journey, both wheels developed slow punctures. You gradually decelerated until you ground to a halt. You had to stop to pump up the tyres. Not only that, you had to buy replacement inner tubes from the bicycle manufacturer every three or four trips.

No-one would stand for it. Or would they?

Remember that the bag is, hitherto, the only way of separating dust and air, then collecting the dust, which is the central function of any vacuum cleaner. Our man pulls apart the machine, and by a series of experiments, discovers that the deterioration is due to the membrane of the bag becoming clogged with dust. Emptying a bag of its cargo of dust and reusing it made little difference, because you can't empty the dust that congests the walls of the bag.

The idea that your hoover lost suction because the bag was full was baloney. Convenient baloney, because you would then go and buy a replacement bag from the manufacturer. It's a tyre with a permanent slow puncture. Cue Dysonian rage at the malevolence and indifference of manufacturers, the gullibility of consumers and the general offence to basic engineering progress.

The observation occurs by chance, which, of course, favours the prepared mind. Ballbarrow production involved spraying the barrows with epoxy powder that would melt when baked and become a protective layer. Much of this spray would miss, and be removed by a large vacuuming contraption. A little research revealed that heavy duty industries with this problem used a cyclone—a cone that centrifugally span dust out of the air. Dyson, in a quite beautiful metaphor of his whole approach, visits the local saw mill under cover of darkness and proceeds to clamber over, sketch and understand the cyclone. The connection with this and his domestic cleaning problem is made, a miniature cardboard cyclone is rigged up and attached to the existing machine. It works.

1979: The loneliness of the long-distance runner
Of the many morals of this story, one we can draw is that innovation is not a sprint. It's a marathon. It wears you down, which is one reason why so few people seriously engage in it. They haven't done the training.

Broke, but with his zeal renewed, Dyson turned to his mentor and former employer Jeremy Fry. By selling part of his land and putting his home up for security, £25,000 was raised, which Fry matched. And so to the Coach House, the hub of Dyson mythology. An outbuilding of his home, this was where Dyson spent most of the following three years testing, rebuilding and prototyping the cyclone technology.

This dogged pursuit of perfection had its consequences. The machine now worked, but the years of development had eaten into reserves, and the plan for the company to manufacture the cleaner was abandoned in favour of a licensing route. Should this work, Dyson and Fry, now Prototypes Limited, could sell the production licence for a fat fee, take a long revenue stream of royalties and return to their drawing boards to invent anew. Should it work.

All they had to do was sell the idea. With Fry a sleeping partner, it was up to Dyson to do the rounds, much as he had successfully done with the Sea Truck and the Ballbarrow.

He ran aground. Again and again. According to his version of events, Dyson would excitedly enter the portals of the great manufacturing businesses of Europe and the US, his revolutionary prototype under his arm, and meet lots of people with nothing under their arms but hair. He spent the next three years failing to make a deal.

The list of companies who met Dyson, then rejected him out of hand, or would not sign an equitable licensing deal, is instructive. Hoover didn't want to speak. (They didn't want to speak to me either.) Hotpoint declined, declaring that the project "was dead from the neck up." Electrolux, Goblin, Black & Decker, Zanussi, Electrostar, AEG, Vax, Hamilton Beach, Amway. It was a roll call of the great and good of the 1980s domestic appliances industry.

Some of them were, in retrospect, just a bit ignorant. A recent review dismissed a new car model as "the answer to a question no-one was asking." And for most of these companies, this just didn't compute. Bags were fine. They were the only game in town. In fact, they made nice money.* This cyclone thing could conceivably work, but who knew, and how would they sell it to a sceptical public?

At some of these businesses, Dyson, with a combination of conviction, charm and demonstration, would reel in a fan. They would like him, see the possibilities and usher the idea through the business. Things would progress until, at some point, someone with a different agenda took over and things would be aborted, or the licensing negotiations would stall because they would not, or could not, meet Dyson's terms.

At others, there was plain skullduggery. In a painful replay of the Ballbarrow experience, Amway, the huge US conglomerate, brought out a copycat version, after terminating an initial licence with Dyson. Electrostar brought a "Zyclon" to the market a few years after dismissing the representative from Prototypes Limited.

The behaviour of these corporations is interesting. In narrative terms, they are useful to the Dyson story, because if you are trying to right a wrong, you need wrongdoers. These behemoths fit the picture. But a business is like any organism. Its principal, overriding ambition is to survive. To do so, it defends itself against threats. Animals are equipped to do this physically. Humans have taught themselves the skills of defending themselves against threatening ideas. Organizations do this by forming a perspective of what they do (their market,

* The bag replacement market in the UK alone was nearly £100m. Multiply that by at least ten for the US. It's not dissimilar to the Microsoft strategy of locking you in and selling you upgrades for eternity.

customers or skills) and systematically excluding things that don't fit this view. That's their version of how they survive. It's a fine balance. Without a strong focus, a business can become wayward, diluting itself. With too narrow a definition of itself, a business can become immune to the feedback and opportunities that the environment offers. Everything defers to the survival instinct of the business.

An individual within a large organization must also have their own survival strategy. This is not normally helped by noisily championing a project of which their superiors are suspicious. Backers fall away.

What is fascinating in all of this is the way Dyson just doesn't get these people and they just don't get him. A source from one of the US companies says:

> **"Actually what I heard was that we could have done a deal, we could have made the numbers add up. But what really killed it was that James Dyson just annoyed people . . . it was the arrogance of the guy and his conviction that he was always right. The people here got the idea, but they couldn't face the thought of working with him. I think that's really why we missed that opportunity."** [17]

Post-rationalizing a failed deal more of more than 20 years ago? Possibly. But confrontation also reveals our uniquely human ability to believe that we are both in the right. Joel Bakan has recently demonstrated that many corporations conform to the clinical definition of a psychopath.[18] As legal entities they answer only to their shareholders, upon whom they depend for survival. They therefore experience no genuine sense of responsibility for their physical environment or the side effects of their products. People who are not shareholders—partners, customers, even employees—are marginalized. And that lowest of the low, the potential supplier flouncing around with his allegedly superior product, doesn't make the frame.

Whether through lack of chemistry, ignorance or nefariousness, no-one teamed up with Prototypes Limited. In typical 1980s fashion, it was the Japanese who saw the opportunity. A luxury import company called Apex were the only people to respond to a feature in a design magazine. Dyson camped in Tokyo for a year, overseeing the manufacture and design, and the G-Force was born. This wasn't quite the approach anyone had envisaged. Apex sold Filofaxes and luxury watches to the nouveau riche of Japan, and, retailing at an astonishing £1,200 a pop, this pink and lavender upright beauty was another piece of conspicuous consumption. Nobody is quite sure whether people actually used it much. Because of the small size of dwellings and the lack of carpets, most Japanese homes had small cylinder cleaners. But it looked the business. It had to: since most homes had virtually no storage space, it was, well, on display.

The Apex deal was well-timed. Struggling under the weight of a business and personal overdraft, and the costs of unravelling the Amway deal, Dyson's family was feeling the strain of his six-year obsession. To understand the financial position you have to understand that Dyson was haemorrhaging at least a quarter of a million pounds a year in legal fees. A guaranteed £60,000 per year was welcome. But it took another three years—until 1990—and another two big deals in the US, with

The G-Force

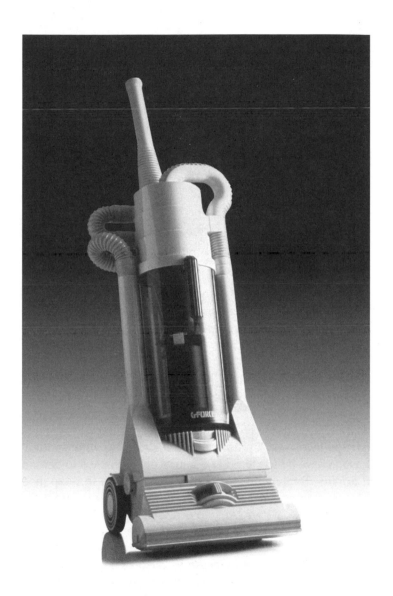

Iona and Johnson Wax, to ease the money troubles. Mind you, let's not get too teary. Dyson and his family continued to live a very nice life, with homes in Bath and Chelsea.

At this point, we need to note the different forms of stamina that were needed.

The first is the stamina of the inventor—the constant retesting, and the constant near misses as he iterates his way to a solution (1979–82).

The second is the stamina of the marketer and salesman. The miles travelled; the cynical responses; the never ending negotiations (1982–87).

The third is the stamina of the litigator (1986–91). This is possibly the most oppressive and testing. It also gets to the root of the actual fight that Dyson is conducting—the fight for the rights to his inventions and, of course, the fruits of them.

Patents and their protection are a war zone, where the only guaranteed beneficiaries are the government, to whom you pay a registration fee, sometimes annually; and patent lawyers, who help you get approval, then defend or attack the various parties involved. A patent holder comes up with an idea, pays to have it registered and approved, then pays to defend it against those who would dispute it. Given the expense of the whole process, those with deeper pockets and more expensive lawyers are likely to prevail. Litigation under these circumstances takes *cojones*.

By 1991 then, something close to Dyson's original ambition was being realized. He worked with a close knit team in Bath, and royalties from the Japanese and American markets were coming in. A flirtation with Vax, the UK-based manufacturer that had done extremely well with its wet and dry machine, led to the customary arguments and law suit.

It was at this point the critical decision came: to move from being an engineer–designer to becoming a manufacturer again. Dyson's two big projects before this had been the Sea Truck and Ballbarrow: in both, he had supervised design, manufacturing and sales.

The move to producing the cleaner was not inevitable. Capital costs prohibited setting up production in the US or Japan, so a licensing route was natural. Even in the UK, the preferred approach—one pursued for nearly ten years—was to have someone else make and sell the product. Dyson's own version of the decision is that characteristic mix of irascibility and energy. He was so pissed off with everyone else failing to make progress, he decided to make the thing himself. What enabled him to do this was the final laying down of legal swords with Amway in the US, plugging the stream of money going towards litigation. Had that agreement not been made, it's unlikely we would have a Dyson brand and business anything like the one we see now.

Of course, raising the funds wasn't straightforward. In fact, the autobiography and subsequent press interviews excoriate the bean counters, merchant banks, venture capitalists, civil servants and ministers of state who failed to stump up in support of the project. The tone, despite Dyson's customary public charm, is that of the sitcom character with his head in his hands, yelling, "Am I surrounded by idiots?" The costs of setting up, principally those of the moulds for the parts, were met by a loan secured on his properties and by selling the rights to the licence for the G-Force in Japan.

Even then, the manufacture had to be sub-contracted, leading to contract disputes, suits and counter-suits. However, once installed in a makeshift factory in Chippenham, and with orders coming through from some of the second division electrical retailers in the UK, momentum started to build throughout 1993 and 1994. The DC01 was an upright vacuum cleaner retailing at twice the price of most competitors. A river of orders became a flood, as the two key UK retailers, Comet and Currys, took the DC01.

> **"A vacuum cleaner designed entirely by me, incorporating innovations up to the very latest point at which my technology had arrived, to be produced and marketed and sold under my own exclusive direction was, to be frank, what this whole thing had been all about."** [19]

So there you have it.

Chapter 5
The Entrepreneur's Story

"Success is the ability to go from one failure to another with no loss of enthusiasm."

Winston Churchill

I meet John Kearon in a small bistro just off London's Oxford Street. John is the owner and founder of BrainJuicer, the fastest growing online market research agency in Europe. (We used them to conduct the research in Chapter 2). He's smart, engaging and wry: you like this man within minutes.

Kearon's upbringing was conventional, even institutional: an army family, university and an early career with Unilever. Compelled to venture outside, he worked in advertising before starting a firm called Brand Genetics. His fascination wasn't so much with marketing, the field in which he worked, but with evolution and ecology. He developed a perspective that looked at organizations and markets much as a naturalist would look at animal life. Ideas, brands and companies thrive or decline in particular environments, just as a population of animals will prosper in one area but die out in another.

Using a Darwinian frame of mind is radical, just as it was when Michael Hannan and John Freeman of Cornell University applied it to organizational theory in the early 1990s. Radical, because it argues that change takes place by the growth of new ideas emerging in unexpected ways, rather than by the intended reform of what exists. Life is much more haphazard than we can ever plan for. We can't really predict what will be fit for a given environment: all we can do is experiment and try, with the sober realization that much of what we do will fail, subject to selection pressures that we cannot predict or control.

Kearon tried to apply this perspective with marketing clients, but eventually tired, since he felt he had ended up in the entertainment business, doing clever analyses for clever people who wouldn't or couldn't embrace the revolutionary import of what was going on. "Managed innovation," a mainstay of most marketing organizations is, by this light, an oxymoron. The interesting things happen on the fringes, as anthropologist and natural historian Gregory Bateson noted. You can't successfully manage innovation any more than you can manage the weather. You can increase your chances of success by great ideas, flexibility, discipline and excellent feedback from the environment, but you can't guarantee anything.

Kearon recalls, in 1999, explaining to one of Unilever's main board directors the results of his analysis of the company's recent innovation record. This showed that around 70 percent of Unilever's profits came from brands that had created a new category such as Birds Eye (the first frozen food), Comfort (the first fabric conditioner), Cif (the first non-scratch cleaner), Dove (the first moisturizing soap), Impulse (the first body spray), Viennetta (the first ice-cream dessert), Magnum (the first super-premium adult impulse ice cream). Significantly, these brands had all originated at the fringes of Unilever's decentralized, federal structure well before the introduction, years earlier, of Unilever's much vaunted and copied Innovation Centres.

The logic of concentrating resources and talent on the important business of innovation seems faultless to large companies used to economy-of-scale thinking. But the fact was that since their introduction Unilever had failed to create any new category brands and the company's return on innovation had significantly decreased. Kearon's point was that just Bateson noted, innovation happens at the fringes, and that Unilever were unwilling to recognize that its old structure had been a much more fertile environment for profitable innovation.

There is even evidence for this at a country level: islands or isolated countries such as the UK, Japan and Israel produce many more patents per head than the large landmass countries such as the US and the old USSR economies.

The Unilever director didn't argue with the statistics but refused to acknowledge that innovation centres weren't a better way. Six years on Unilever's innovation and financial performance continues to disappoint.

Kearon's mind continued to conflate evolutionary theory and marketing. And a chink of light emerged, especially when he began to see the world wide web as a fertile testing ground for ideas and opinions. Surely, with the appropriate technology, marketers could access minds across the globe, allowing them to generate and test ideas for their fitness and see what emerged. We could mimic the patterns of mutation and selection in nature. What was needed was a way of doing this.

There was sacrifice involved. Kearon had a family to feed, and often felt on the "toehold of existence" as he pursued the idea. After two years in the spare bedroom ("a scary and lonely place") and a lot of false starts, the idea of BrainJuicer— a fast, smart, informal way of market research emerged. The distinctive feature of the research is what's called a "Mind Reader." This has the premise that we understand things by association. I understand the idea of a brother-in-law by reference to a brother, which in turn I understand by reference to the idea of a family.

Everything we know is built up of particles of knowledge attaching themselves to one another and becoming clusters, or being detached if they are of no use. It is mutation and selection in action. Given this, we can understand people's perceptions better if we successively ask them for their associations with a particular topic and disaggregate them (as on page 34) and if we have others build up their own responses using the language and ideas that have gone before in the survey. So, if I am the first to respond to a Mind Reader, I make up my own associations with the topic. If I'm 50th to do the survey, I'm able to make use of the associations mentioned by the preceding 49 people. It's evolution in action, but this time in the form of market research.

Specifically, the research is powered by a patented algorithm. It's a machine. The entrepreneur's interest is in moving from speculation to something tangible, while others just speculate.

There are several parallels with Dyson's story, and indeed John cites Dyson as an inspiration during tough times. There is the intense curiosity in a particular problem or field that seems to be substandard (for Kearon, research methods, for Dyson, the vacuum cleaner). There is the willingness to pursue and the enjoyment of pursuing paths contrary to conventional wisdom and doing business. And there is the psychological requirement to pioneer. I am compelled to do stuff like this, says Kearon. And my main motivation for making money is that I can get lots of cash to play some more.

What you've just read is a story: that of John Kearon and BrainJuicer, within a larger story, that of James Dyson and his company. I'd like, in this chapter, to explore why these stories have power and meaning for us.

As a species, we have a deep need for explanatory and descriptive accounts of how we came to be, how we should behave and what our path should be. We call these stories. A typical Western form is that made famous by the extraordinary Joseph Campbell book—*The Hero With A Thousand Faces.*[20] Essentially, Campbell made explicit the patterns that unite many thousands of stories and myths across time, culture and continents. Consistently, stories feature a central protagonist who is drawn away from their "ordinary world" by a call to adventure. They are often encouraged by a mentor and engage in a series of tests and ordeals in order to claim something of fundamental importance to them. They take possession of this and return to the world, more complete and with new knowledge or boons to share with others. The most universally successful films of recent years—*Toy Story, Finding Nemo, Shrek, Star Wars, Lord of the Rings*—rely explicitly on this formula. What has been lost must be found, through the agency of a protagonist—someone who combines commitment and vulnerability in their search for resolution. In reading or viewing the story, we take on the qualities of the protagonist.

The pattern is symbolic of each person's struggle for psychological wholeness. To become more of who we are, we must stretch beyond ourselves, engage in conflict and hardship, and thereby become richer in wisdom and experience. In life, of course, there is never just one journey. We continue to cycle through the pattern. The stories exist as constant reminders of what is possible, should we but try.

Societies encourage and develop different versions of the hero's journey. Military-based cultures have warriors as heroes who best the enemy in order to bring home the reward of land and honour. Religions have powerful narratives describing how individual figures demonstrate faith in impossible or implausible circumstances, with the rewards of immortality beckoning. Capitalist economies require the consistent trial and error of business start ups in order to thrive. They have developed their own subgenre of the hero myth —The Entrepreneur's Journey.

Before we look at this in more detail, let's become more familiar with the pattern established by Campbell, and later developed by Christopher Vogler, whose terminology I will use here. [21]

There is an ordinary world in which the protagonist exists, when they hear and respond to a call to adventure. They are reluctant and may refuse the call. Encouraged by a mentor, they cross a threshold into a new world, where they meet with tests, allies and enemies. They approach an inmost cave, where a great ordeal awaits, before taking possession of a reward. They are pursued on the road back to their own world, and cross a final threshold, experiencing resurrection, and being transformed by the experience, before they return with the elixir.

In researching this book, I came across a perfect example of the genre—*How I Made It*, a collection of *Sunday Times* columns that describes and celebrates successful entrepreneurs. The grandaddy of celebrity entrepreneurs, Richard Branson, is on the front cover, endorsing with gusto.

The stories have a typical pattern. An individual becomes discontented with their current job or status (the ordinary world). A chance observation or opportunity motivates them to experiment with starting a business (call to adventure). They find backers or a partner (the mentor). They cross the threshold into their own enterprise and embark upon a series of tests, reversals and ordeals. There is often a pivotal test or ordeal, which challenges the protagonist's values and resolve. Having laid claim to the reward, the protagonist eventually returns to their starting place, psychologically wiser and with the boon of greater wealth as a reward for their endeavour.

Here's another story—that of Harry Cragoe, the founder of PJ Smoothies, the company that makes, well, smoothies. Cragoe had worked successively as a commodity broker and then as a partner in another venture. He recalls being unfit, pasty and white (the ordinary world). Business took him to Venice, Los Angeles. He became enamoured of the lifestyle, the focus on health and developed a taste for smoothies from the local juice bars. He became a believer (call to adventure). He persuaded a friend, Patrick Folkes (mentor), to join forces with him, and together they crossed the threshold—the symbolic sale of all his possessions in order to raise finance.

The journey was embarked upon and with it a series of tests, reversals and ordeals. No juice manufacturers in the UK were prepared to back the enterprise. Their only option was to source frozen product in the US, then ship it to the UK to be packaged. They hawked their product around hundreds of outlets in London, eventually selling some in a West London supermarket—on a freezing cold day in December, not the ideal time for smoothies.

They grew, but realized they needed control of the product, eventually deciding to manufacture it themselves. They took on the overheads and risk of employment and were close to breaking point when their sole distributor went into bankruptcy. Contracts with the major supermarkets put the business onto a more sustainable footing. The days of breadline living over,

Cragoe could now draw a good income from a business turning over millions of pounds (reward) but his ambitions remained high. His sights are now set on children's drinks—and there are an awful lot of people not yet drinking PJ Smoothies. [22]

Implicitly or explicitly, all hero's journey stories bring us face to face with our own mortality, and what we do in its presence. The form asks us to consider our response when confronted with danger. In traditional forms of the tale, the protagonist dices with literal death. He faces Goliath, the lions in the arena, the enemy swordsman, the dragon—and in doing so slays the demons within. It demonstrates the willingness to risk death in the face of a belief.

In our entrepreneurial narratives, death is symbolized by the failure of the business. A lack of money or bankruptcy stands for death. There is the attendant spectre of shame, either personal or social, stemming from the failure. There are critical moments of stress (when Cragoe's distributor failed; when Dyson was failing to get backing for production in 1992) but the entrepreneur's is more of a chronic ordeal. Financial "death" is never far away, and the persistent stress of overdrafts, bank negotiations and the possibility of failure can be consuming.

The writer and consultant to small businesses Michael Gerber, author of *The E Myth Revisited*,[23] is explicit in his belief that creating a business is a deliberate act of psychological adventure. In doing so, you are putting yourself in jeopardy, creating an experiment in which you are the main subject, and putting to the test your self-knowledge, your strength and your vulnerability. By opening up shop, you are opening up to the world. You can't hide any more. You will know if you can actually sell, manage or produce something. You will know if your idea is real or a fantasy. You will know, under the unique stress of self-employment, how you behave when much more than just a job is at stake. Opening a business is like opening a theatre, except you are the one under the lights.

The Dyson story

The capsule Dyson story is a powerful summary of the hero's journey. I left behind security and income to pursue an idea of a better vacuum cleaner. After thousands of hours and attempts and in terrible debt, I launched the Dual Cyclone in the UK on a wing and a prayer, sustained by my belief in a better product. I now run a multi-million pound organization and am engaged in innovation in a range of categories.

Intriguingly though, the vacuum cleaner is but a fractal of the larger story of Dyson's life and business, as we see in the following table, where the first column represents the stages of the journey, the second the story of the cleaner, and the third the larger story.

As I hope I've demonstrated, the Dyson story is satisfying because it conforms to archetypal patterns. Dysons sell for two reasons. We buy a product: one that cleans well, and endows the user with a sense of competence. We also buy an idea: the belief that the world can be made better by human ingenuity as embodied by a figure who achieves recognition and wealth as a reward.

The steps of the hero's journey	The vacuum cleaner story	The larger story
The ordinary world There is an ordinary, mundane world in which the protagonist exists.	Having been forced out of the Kirk-Dyson (Ballbarrow) business, Dyson is left metaphorically kicking his heels. He is at home, vaguely disconsolate.	James Dyson's childhood and schooling: the talented, directionless and peculiarly stubborn boy, already allergic to institutions and convention. The family expectation is that he becomes a teacher, doctor or professional.
The call to adventure A problem, challenge or adventure is undertaken.	He strips down the Hoover Junior in an attempt to understand its poor performance. Contemporaneously, he's introduced to the idea of the cyclone and clambers across the saw mill at night. A cardboard and gaffer tape prototype is knocked up. It's time to right a wrong, and possible make a fortune in the process.	Art school in London, where he encounters the worlds of industrial and product design, and is entranced by their possibilities, as well as the hero-figures who have bestrode engineering, such as Brunel.
The refusal of the call The protagonist balks at the scale of the venture, experiencing fear.	Dyson records no explicit fears at the outset, but we can imagine the concerns: low income, big overdraft, great uncertainty. During the 80s, he will experience the chronic entrepreneurial brushes with bankruptcy.	The natural anxiety that accompanies any new venture and risk taking.
Meeting with the mentor An encounter with a figure who helps prepare the protagonist for the unknown.	Turns to his previous mentor, Jeremy Fry, who helps him form a company and provides seed investment.	A series of male mentor figures, at college and in early years. Notably Jeremy Fry, the millionaire founder of Rotork, with whom Dyson deeply identified and who had trod the innovator–entrepreneur path before him.

The steps of the hero's journey	The vacuum cleaner story	The larger story
Crossing the first threshold When the action gets going.	Three years in the Coach House, testing thousands of prototypes and developing a working Dual Cyclone.	At a very young age, being taken on by Fry to develop and design the Sea Truck in a form of apprenticeship.
Tests, allies, enemies A series of encounters, in which the protagonist begins to learn the rules of the different or special world.	The adventures of the 1980s, clashing with a series of industry "enemies" who refuse to recognize or license the idea.

Temporary relief as the licence in Japan is sold to Apex and the G-Force is born. | The successive ventures of the Sea Truck, the Ballbarrow and the vacuum cleaner businesses.* The increasing endorsement of an alternative way of doing business: to invent, manufacture and market yourself, rather than rely on the conventions of big business and marketing trickery. |
| **Approach to the inmost cave** The hero comes close to the object of the quest—the place where reward is, and where danger must be confronted. | The "inmost cave" here is to manufacture the machine himself, rather than simply license the technology. (As he had done with both the Sea Truck and Ballbarrow). This entails raising funds borrowed against his property, and the security of his family at risk. | Arguably, in the narrative of the Dyson business, this is the decision to set up and export directly to the US.

Only in the biggest market in the world will the idea finally be proven: only here will it (and the founder) be fully recognized.

And of course, this is the backyard of the big beasts: Hoover, Amway, Black & Decker. The warrior needs to best them. |

*The law of three. As Christopher Booker notes, there is an insistent recurrence of the pattern of three in stories. "Three in stories is the number of growth and transformation." The pattern in the Dyson story is the "ascending three," where each thing is of value, but a little more than the last. The ascending three is depicted symbolically in the three treasures Jack wins from the giant, or the familiar pattern of bronze, silver and gold.

The steps of the hero's journey

The vacuum cleaner story

The larger story

Ordeal
Where the fortunes of the protagonist hit rock bottom, he faces death or defeat —and his own fears. This is the moment of greatest jeopardy.

There are multiple risks in the early 1990s. But the key, extended ordeal, is the move from contracted to in-house manufacture, which nearly unravels the business, with all the capital funds exhausted.

The move to the US forces the decision to outsource manufacturing to Asia. The golden boy of UK industry is suddenly tarnished, and, symbolically, is abandoning the world that he has fostered. He has to bow to the rules, rather than break them again.

The robotic cleaner and washing machine ventures struggle to make any commercial headway.

Reward
The protagonist takes possession of the treasure he or she has come seeking.

Symbolically, this is the first DC01 coming off the production lines at Chippenham. Practically, it is the sales success of the DC01 in the home market of the UK.

Success in the US, not just financially, but in the way the founder and brand are embraced by the culture.

The road back
It's not over. The forces who have been defeated will not rest still and they come after the hero.

The vacuum cleaner industry does not rest. It comes out with copycat models. It thwarts the Dyson business wherever it can find it (UK, France, Germany).

The intense competitiveness of the floor care business remains.

The jury is still out on whether the Dyson business can be more than a vacuum cleaner company, despite its ambitions.

Resurrection
There is often a final life-or-death moment, when the antagonistic forces must be defeated again. Vogler calls this a "kind of final exam for the hero."

Symbolically, for the vacuum cleaner business, this was the 1999-2001 court case, where Dyson sued Hoover Europe for infringement of its patent rights, after Hoover brought out the Triple Vortex model.

No-one, of course, knows what awaits the business, except similar tests, ordeals and rewards.

Return with the elixir
The protagonist returns, but the return is empty without the gift or "elixir." This may be treasure, but is often knowledge, freedom, love or wisdom.

The elixir, in the case of this protagonist, is the recognition that a new way of doing business can thrive, even in the face of challenge and cynicism. David can triumph over Goliath, because David's got the better kit.

Chapter 6
Growing Up and Going Abroad: 1997–2005

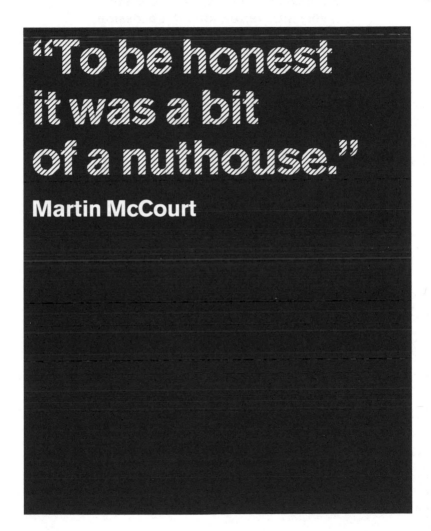

"To be honest it was a bit of a nuthouse."

Martin McCourt

". . . there was no-one to teach me how to run. There was no dad to tell me how great I was, and it became a very introverted kind of obsession with me . . . I would get up at six in the morning and run in the wilds of Norfolk for hours, or put on my running kit at ten o'clock at night and not reappear till after midnight . . . and I knew that I was training myself to do something better than anyone else would be able to." [24]
James Dyson, *Against The Odds*, describing a period of adolescence

In the UK, sales continued to rise, and by 1997, Dyson, aided by the launch of its first cylinder model, the DC02, in 1995, had a dominant market share, a position it still holds at the time of writing. We need to recognize that these sorts of rapid transformations, especially in established markets, are very rare. The relatively stable world of domestic appliances had never seen anything like it. A parallel would be a new brand of cooker, using a different fuel or cooking method going from nothing to market leader in three years. Even technology-driven brands such as the Sony PlayStation or Apple iPod are not really displacing existing players—they are creating new markets of their own.

Parallels with the Dyson stump my local Currys manager. "It's sort of done to hoovers what George Foreman Grills have done to sandwich makers." That's an imperfect analogy, but it's the best he can do.

The DC02

The world of the domestic appliance industry was, and is, a strange one. It's a little dull on one hand and brutally competitive on the other.

Televisions, for example, a mainstay of a retailer like Comet in the UK, or Best Buy in the US, are a horrible market to be in, with its remorseless cost pressures and concentration of buying power.

A lot of domestic appliance executives spend a lot of time wondering whether they should even be in the industry. Surely, the grief would be less and the returns more somewhere else?

The rules of the unloved market
These circumstances create what we might call an unloved market. Everyone tends to be constrained by an assumed set of rules, the primary one being that this is about as good as it's going to get. The manufacturers struggle to make any money, incur the ill will of their shareholders and senior executives and resent the buying power of the retailers. The retailers give us stores (certainly in my experience in the UK and US) that are empty of any form of excitement, theatre or even modest interest. When did you last meet a member of staff who seemed interested in what he was selling you, despite the fact it might be a sale of hundreds of pounds, euros or dollars? The basic forms and technologies of much of what they're selling—refrigerators, washing machines, cookers, hobs, heaters—have changed very little over the past decades.

What you end up with is a routine line up of products from cash-constrained producers, sold by retailers in soul-less environments to customers who'd rather be somewhere else.

In the 1960s and 70s the vacuum cleaner market had a different form. Much of the distribution was through generalist and department stores. Demonstrators, employed by the manufacturers, were a common sight on the shop floors, often in competition. This gave the sense of a market and a sense of occasion. The brands were physically represented by people who knew about the product. There was conversation and interest.

In the late 1970s, Goblin, a licensee of Millers in the US, had developed the wet pick-up feature and incorporated it into regular cleaners. It galloped to over 50 percent of the UK market by the early 1980s. It also managed to make the market deeply unprofitable by its high-volume, low-price strategy. It's another of those unfortunate stories where a manufacturer unwittingly cripples itself through over supply. (You'll find car industry executives at the local employment exchange who'll explain exactly how the process works.) When Dyson approached Goblin in the mid-1980s, its sales force was on an enforced two-day week.

Throughout the 1970s, the market became rapidly commoditized, with an exception we'll look at in a moment. Price, discounting and promotional offers become the norm, rather than any systematic attempt to explain the different virtues of the products on offer. Within this system, everyone trains each other to have low expectations and lower prices. It's a form of mutually reinforcing banality.

When a new entrant comes into a system like this, the effects can be significant. It projects an attractive confidence about its own offer and in doing so raises the status of the category. In the words of the song, it doesn't have to be this way. In a sister edition of this book, John Simmons' *My Sister's a Barista*, we discover how much of Starbucks' early success was down to its sheer enthusiasm about the virtues of coffee. That sort of verve and confidence is compelling, especially when many others in the market appear to have downgraded the product and their efforts. If you're from the UK or US, can you remember trying to get a reasonable cup of coffee before 1990? That's what I mean. Precisely these circumstances affected the vacuum category in the UK.

Disruption
Enter, not Dyson, but Vax.

Vax was a British manufacturer, also based in the west of England. Led by Alan Brazier, its principal innovation was to market the twin features of wet and dry cleaning in a single machine to the retail market. Don't just vacuum your carpet, it said. Clean it.

The value of this shouldn't be underestimated. Carpet cleaning was an expensive and demanding business. A machine with the promise of really coming to grips with domestic dust and dirt was compelling. Brazier had taken the wet-pick-up idea one step further and through his knowledge of the commercial cleaning market recognized the value of "washing" carpets. He invented a simple cleaning head that would both dispense and pick up water. He also recognized the need to demonstrate such an idea and made the cleaning head from clear plastic. Vax benefitted from the distinctive user experience that Dyson would later employ to great effect. You could see all the crap: in this case, the muddy or discoloured water issuing from your carpet.

The disruptive effect of Vax broke the hold of Hoover, Electrolux and Goblin over the UK market in two ways. First, Vax sold very well, creating the domestic wet–dry sector and taking big chunks of market share from the incumbents. At its peak, at the end of the 1980s, Vax had over 50 percent of the market in terms of value. Second, it reshaped the way people saw the market. It took the price above £100 for the first time. It gave a renewed prominence to technology, attuning buyers to the possibility of difference. And its products were distinctively designed: in an orange and black that was pretty unmistakeable. As Graham Capron-Tee, a seasoned industry observer comments, it was the first modern brand in the sector—the first to sell an idea, rather than just sell another vacuum cleaner. [25]

Vax had the sort of sustained commercial effect that Dyson would later enjoy. What it never achieved was the same cultural status.

The DC01 and its inventor were, somehow, utterly of their time. By 2000, they had passed into the vernacular. "Doing a Dyson" meant that you invented and made your own product. Buttressed by its huge commercial success, the DC01 entered design museums and exhibitions. Politicians jumped in, citing the company as a working model of the best of British engineering and endeavour. The product's appeal was widespread, but its cost and aesthetics took it more naturally to an up-market audience, and it slotted in as part of the domestic discourse of the chattering classes.

Inside the phenomenon

By all accounts, Dyson in the late 1990s was a heady place to be. Current and former employees describe the pace like this:

"It was a bit like being on a runaway horse. It's exciting stuff, but you always think you're about to be thrown off. In fact, you know you're going to be thrown off—it's just a matter of when!" [26]

Typically, a company will be stretched in this adolescent growth phase in several directions. Growth demands a new maturity in dealing with people, new management skills and systems that can cope with the rising tide of orders, logistics and technical quirks.

The business had three principal challenges. First: could it actually manufacture and deliver its product to the quality and in the quantity needed? Second: could it continue to drive new ideas and technology, the lifeblood of its future? Third: could it go international?

Let's look at the third challenge first. In licensing the dual cyclone technology to Japan, and subsequently the US, Dyson had confirmed his instinct: he had a solution to a universal need. All the world was bagged up, and that was an opportunity. With the plateau of UK sales in sight, and the US licence taken, mainland Europe was the obvious first step.

So, Australia it was. Ross Cameron was a career engineer and manager at SC Johnson, which had taken the commercial cleaning licence in North America. At one of the many pitch meetings he had been struck by "this English character with a bagless vacuum cleaner, who clearly thought his upright was the greatest thing since sliced bread." [27] A rational and methodical figure, he had caught the

Dyson bug. His understanding of the Australian market, his engineer's appreciation of the technology and his simple love of the iconic product led him to lead the first official sortie abroad by Dyson Appliances in 1995–6.

Cameron and his team developed the template for moving into a country. Broadly, this consisted of gales of enthusiasm and technical support from Malmesbury, and not a whole lot else. A founder who launched on a shoestring is not in the habit of ladling money out to fledgling foreign operations. Left largely to his own devices, Cameron deployed word of mouth and product placement to create early conviction, but accompanied this with a thoroughly orderly approach to training and getting after sales service in place.

Australia is, in many ways, a thoroughly conservative society. Outside Sydney's central suburbs, its domestic appliance retailers felt both apprehensive and suspicious about the DC01. Rather like the UK had been, the market was anaesthetized by cheap prices and big brand machines with bells and whistles. "You'll last about six months," offered one of the more complimentary buyers. Cameron couldn't even be sure of that. David Jones, the Melbourne retailer, took 150 machines in June 1996, but Dyson Australia chewed its nails for the remainder of the winter until a big October order kick-started the business.

With the wind in its favour, it became apparent that the strategy followed in the UK could work. The product was placed with key journalists, who wrote enthusiastically about it and its refreshingly unstuffy Pom inventor. The market debate was quickly stirred up, with the classic challenger strategy of unmasking the laziness and folly of the main players.

Alongside this was investment in after-care, with the intent that any issues or support required after purchase would be routed through to Dyson, rather than the retailer taking the load. Cameron and his team also paid enormous amounts of attention to the training and motivation of the retailers' staff. Within three years, Dyson had over 50 percent of the Australian market by value. The combination of assertive public relations, trade focus and product performance had worked its magic.

The French subsidiary was launched in 1996 and Germany and Spain in 1997. The brief from Malmesbury was to get going and to make it work. The founder appears to have swept a lot of caution aside in this period. His desire to move into selling in Western Europe is variously described as infectious and insanely driven by those around at the time. The business was intent on launching multiple operations in Europe while its factory struggled to meet UK orders. Growth left much of the rest of the operation running on vapour.

"To be honest, it was a bit of a nuthouse"

These are the engaging words of Martin McCourt, the CEO of Dyson Appliances, who joined Dyson in 1996. The recruitment interview process was instructive.

> **"I think we argued most of the hour and a half. I found James pretty confrontational. I met some other people who were less argumentative but he was dead argumentative. I remember driving back up the motorway thinking 'that's not going to happen.'" [28]**

But happen it did. McCourt joined with the brief of pulling together sales, marketing and exporting, in line with the plan to expand rapidly in Europe. A former employee of Mars, Duracell and Toshiba, he had, like Cameron, spent most of his working life with corporate giants, and he found the sense of exuberance and energy intoxicating. He says he's been pretty much on "alert status" since the day he joined.

When he arrived, demand for the product was great, but a lot of other things weren't. Like many rapidly growing companies, the basic business architecture was built around a "small" product or service. As the enterprise took off, the primary task—meeting demand—became increasingly strained. Better balance was required.

Companies built on the vision and conviction of a charismatic founder will often require a balancing, complementary figure. The king needs a chief of staff, and a sorter. Bill Gates has Steve Ballmer; Richard Branson has Will Whitehorn; Howard Schultz has Howard Behar. James Dyson has Martin McCourt.

The role of the chief of staff is to contain and direct the energy of the visionary, thereby freeing him to do what he is best at, and making commercial and organizational sense of the whirlwind. McCourt describes his role as being to create space so that James Dyson can get on with what he's great at—namely inventing the technology and applications that will ensure the future off the company.

Publicly, the leader is the spokesperson and embodiment of the business. Just in the shadow of the leading light, however, a figure is always busy managing consequences and expectations. In a charismatically led organization, everyone is trying to understand or second guess the immediate intentions of the founder. Everyone wants to bathe in the light.

> **"There are two questions in everyone's mind at Dyson. One is, 'What would James do here?' which is often liberating, leading you to risk things and challenge the status quo. The other is, 'What would James think of this'— and implicitly, what would he think of me. That's the darker side, because you can never really know."** [29]
> Former employee

So what was it like being the manager, the person who has to impose some control round here? I ask McCourt. "That's a very good question," he smiles. But one he's not about to answer. We can speculate, however, based on the experience of others in a similar position, and the points of view of those who have worked closely with Dyson.

The relationship between manager and founder can be extremely tough. It is, essentially, a relationship of opposites.

Successful entrepreneurs tend to bypass constraints or invent ways out of them. Defiance is how they get their kicks; it drives and defines them. Successful managers, in contrast, tend to impose discipline; their job is to harness the power of entrepreneurs.

To founders, managers symbolize constraints. They are the people brought in to create the order they know must happen— but inwardly resent.

The ideal is for the opposites to complement each other rather than clash. For this to be achieved, managers have to have both a strong belief in the enterprise and a strong sense of self and competence. Without the former, they may tire of the constant challenge. Without the latter, they can be caught up in the dynamic of the founder's drive and lose their sense of direction, becoming embittered or jealous.

The head of a venture capital firm describes this experience: "I was manager to the visionary for a while, and I got jealous. I took over when the founder left, and had to battle with the new manager's envy. Technically, our roles were clear, but the psychology was all over the place."

In a company like Dyson, the relationship has an additional edge. James Dyson and his family are the only shareholders. The founder, chief inventor and only shareholder is a formidable partner with whom to hold your own. But only by doing so do you get respect and legitimacy. In retrospect, McCourt's interview process was symbolic.

Managers are buffers between the leader and their followers. They have to persistently interpret, explain and reassure. Projects have to be curtailed, investments switched and people disappointed. At the same time, they must allow the organization to breathe. In Dyson, it would be easy, given the culture of risk and innovation, to poison the well with bureaucratic ink. It's to the management team's credit that it's been able to establish the necessary controls without denting the direction and purpose of the business. But it's clear this hasn't been without pain.

Production: Adulthood and the loss of innocence

In 2001–02, the business made a decision that marked its transition from adolescence to adulthood. It relocated production from the UK factory near its home base to Malaysia. In doing so it had to lose about 600 people.

It is a decision about which Dyson is sensitive. (It was its main preoccupation when Cyan Books approached it about the book you're reading.) Reading the press at the time, one is struck by the profile of the story. Tony Blair, the UK prime minister expressed his "deep disappointment" in the House of Commons. The reaction in the UK reflected British preoccupations. Running through the commentary is a sense of failure: the latest chapter in the narrative of the decline of British manufacturing. The human consequences of the redundancies were highlighted and implicitly or explicitly compared with the founder's personal wealth. This wasn't the Right Thing. For goodness sake, the Queen had visited the factory only two months before the announcement.

James Dyson, because of the publicity he had courted, got it in the neck. The poster boy for UK industry had turned his back on Britain because he could get Malaysians for a third of the price.

A business journalist who reported on the story at the time recalls:

> **"I think the reason why it got such a profile was the mix of betrayal and relief. He'd led people off to this brave new world, and look what**

**happened. There's that peculiar
British sense of the world being
restored to normality with the
failure of something different."** [30]

First, we should get some context. This was a recessionary
period. In the same month, February 2002, BA announced
5,800 job cuts, Energis 1,300, Smiths Engineering Group
2,000, EMI 1,800. The following month, the Philipp Holzmann
construction firm collapsed, costing 23,000 German jobs, and
Ericsson shed 20,000 jobs across Europe. Meanwhile, in the
US, Levi Strauss fired a fifth of its employees. No-one was
immune from the restructuring of the global economy.

Second, we should not underestimate the trauma that the
decision caused within the business. The Dyson organization
had been built on a strong sense of purpose and mutuality, and
the feeling that its destiny was tied to its leader's. Suddenly,
it became clear that, on a pretty large scale, people were
expendable. Dyson was still going places, but they weren't
going with him any more. Notwithstanding the huge efforts
to redeploy people within the business, or to find them
employment locally, this was a big crack in the dream. It was
bloody, says one insider—the end of innocence.

This phrase is poignant and instructive. Dyson was not a
commercial innocent—anything but. But part of its appeal was
the practised naivety of its offer. This wasn't a company, it was
an activist. It championed the cause of better products and
technology to improve people's lives while kicking the shins of
the big boys. This offer was made to the people in the business,
and it continues today. We're on a mission. People, much more
than in more routine workplaces, have faith in what they are
doing and in each other. But the end of innocence happens

when tough, even necessary, decisions deeply damage the interests of those who had previously considered themselves members of the family. The interests of the corporate concern outweigh those of individuals and we can no longer pretend it is not so.

> **"Asked if he felt any rancour, the manager shrugged. 'If I was in his shoes, it was my business and my money, I'd do the same.'"** [31]
> Reporter interviewing one of the redundant supervisors

Dyson maintains that it made sterling efforts to keep manufacturing in the UK. It tried to expand the existing plant, but met with consistent planning objections. It tested manufacture on other UK sites, but met with scheduling and quality problems. As costs continued to climb and production became bottlenecked, it saw serious problems ahead. Cash was being diverted from development towards patching up operations, which was untenable in the long term. The business felt hobbled.

The internal logic of companies means growth is necessary—to generate cash to try new things, to reward employees and shareholders at increasing levels. James Dyson had a typically jaw-dropping goal. He wanted Dyson to be as big in the US as it was in the UK and he wanted, at the same time, to make a more sustained assault on Europe, where sales growth was unsatisfactory.

This simply couldn't be done out of Malmesbury. Even if the company had been able to expand UK manufacturing, the relative costs and inflexibility would have denied it the financial or production base to crack the American market.

The more research that was done, the more the conclusion became clear. The Far East, and specifically Malaysia, was a much better place to make vacuum cleaners. Overheads per unit were dramatically less. Many suppliers to Dyson (plastics, electrical and motor) had migrated to the East and others were following. The quality regimes and professional standards were higher.

Going to America

The application of cyclone technology wasn't new to the US. Dyson, remember, had licensed it to the Iona Corporation, who had been selling two models, the Fantom and the Lightning, with modest success, but little zeal or innovation. Fortuitously for Dyson, the US business went into bankruptcy in late 2001, and with it its manufacturing licence. (It later reappeared selling cyclonic cleaners, but with copycat technology.)

The move to the US meant Dyson had to perform at a different level. It had to beef up. Its ambition meant that it couldn't trade piecemeal and gradually break through over several years. The US retail structure was becoming concentrated, and the sums only worked if you could break into the likes of Sears, Best Buy, Wal-Mart and Target. But to do so, you had to prove two things—first that your stuff would sell, and second that you had the capacity to trade with the Americans straight away, nationally. There was no "Let's try it in Michigan and see how it goes." The US retail giants haven't got the attention span for that.

Dyson had to have the infrastructure, logistics, stock to cope. That takes money—the kind of savings only possible through the relocation of production to Malaysia.

Like everywhere else, the sell-in was frustrating. The business model of selling a premium-priced product at high volumes didn't compute for the retailers. Their model of value was low prices in huge volumes. The evidence of success in the UK and Australia didn't count for much, since they were, well, quirky, British kinds of places. The investment risks in training staff, support and service were modest, but real.

As before, and since, the product came to the rescue. The dual cyclone had evolved into the Root[8] cyclone. On discovering that multiple cyclones gave better performance (smaller cyclones have a tighter radius, with better separation of dust and air; having more of them creates faster airflow overall) Dyson packed eight into the new models, which were then studded with other improvements.

The important breakthroughs were when two people at Best Buy, one of the large chains, used the upright DC07 at home, and became enthusiasts. They sensed the mass market possibilities. Chance intervened. Internal changes within the buying team allowed them to take a bet on Dyson, leading to an order to supply 600 stores. By September 2002, it was game on. As in the UK in the mid-1990s, astute publicity and product placement created a tipping point beyond which the product flew off shelves. By 2006, Dyson was selling over one million units in the US a year. A feature on *Will and Grace* confirmed its status as part of the US metropolitan zeitgeist.

This is part of an influential technology blog by Jeremy Zawodny, a senior player at Yahoo!:

> **"The first time I used the Dyson, which is bagless, I completely filled the chamber twice. It picked up an amazing amount of cat hair, litter and other tidbits. Based on just that one use, I was sold. This vacuum is far and away the best I've ever used or seen. Not only does it suck really well, it comes with a ton of attachments that make cleaning furniture and stairs fairly easy too. The extension hose is significantly longer than those I've seen on other units."** [32]

In many ways, the marketing mirrored previous approaches: intense work at the ground level to ensure standards and after care, heavy investment in public relations. But a new slant was featuring Dyson himself in advertising. The work was very understated, showing James Dyson in his laboratory explaining his innovation, but perfectly pitched. This was the American dream, but British in flavour.

On February 4, 2006, Maytag, the owner of the Hoover business in North America, put it up for sale. It's the end of another chapter.

Chapter 7
The Productive Narcissist

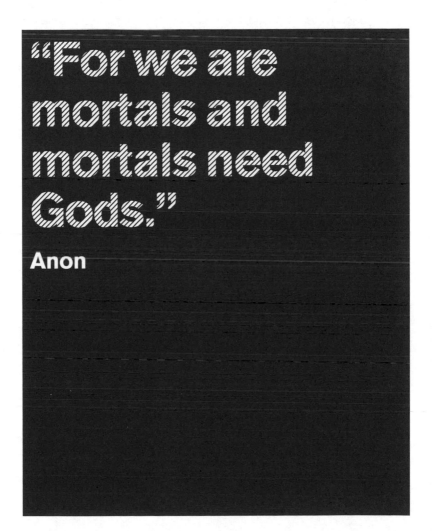

"For we are mortals and mortals need Gods."

Anon

It's early January, and there's still frost on the ground at ten o'clock. I meet Bill Critchley, one of the directors of Ashridge Consulting, in the Elysian surroundings of Ashridge Management College. I've made contact with Bill because he combines a robust consulting approach with a practice as a Gestalt psychotherapist, and I'm intrigued by his experience as a consultant to founder-organizations, such as Dyson (although he's never worked directly with the company). I'm after a little free consulting, frankly, as I process the research and hypotheses kicking around in my head.

We venture into several territories and spend time with Narcissus. This, you will recall, is the Greek myth of the figure who becomes enraptured by his own reflection in a spring at the foot of Mount Helios. In general discourse, the idea of someone who is narcissistic has become a pejorative term, implying self-obsession and vanity.

The author Michael Maccoby has written extensively on this subject in his book *The Productive Narcissist*. Rejecting the usual stereotype of the individual who is destroyed by a preoccupation with himself, Maccoby defines the productive narcissist as the personality type best suited to lead during times of rapid social and economic change. At the same time, he makes clear that narcissistic leadership doesn't always mean successful leadership and that narcissists lacking strategic intelligence are fated to crash and burn. This chapter looks at how James Dyson has managed to combine his own drama and a very high level of strategic intelligence.

In the psychotherapeutic domain, narcissism is used as a way of understanding aspects of a person's energy and drive, and how these have been shaped by earlier circumstances. Critchley has found the idea useful as he works with certain founder-entrepreneurs and their colleagues. He is at pains to say that there are different types of founders, some of whom have no need to advertise themselves or their achievements. A clue is often in the naming of the business: the slightly narcissistic founder will be identified directly with the company. This is why so many advertising agencies are named after the founding partners (Saatchi and Saatchi, Bartle Bogle Hegarty, or, whisper it soft, the Maccoby Group). Agencies and consultancies are, notoriously, theatres of self-publicity and performance anxiety.

> **"It's my experience that the entrepreneur-founder may have something of a narcissistic personality. We only develop a sense of self in relation to others, by being well-mirrored and well-reflected. If that isn't satisfied, or is only partially satisfied, there is a nagging sense of incompleteness . . . You develop a particular survival strategy, and one option is to become remarkable, and inventive . . . You do this in service of the admiration you never got, and being seen in a way you never were."** [33]

In working with the management teams of the more charismatic founders, Critchley notices certain recurrent patterns. Many people are attracted to the founder and their brilliantly embodied belief in an ideal. Their energy and conviction are deeply seductive: they create a light in which people bathe, especially younger people. In a post-modern world, where every idea is up for grabs and where long-held assumptions are melting around us, this form of passionate intensity is both attractive and consoling. We're doing amazing things here. Do you want to come along for the ride?

. It's redolent of that other great productive narcissist Steve Jobs enticing the then Pepsi boss, John Sculley, to Apple, with the words, "Do you want to sell sugared water or do you want to change the world?"

The psychodynamics of organizations

The invitation offered by Jobs is similar to that offered by any charismatic leader; it's important to understand what it means.

The psychodynamics of organizations is a big topic, and we can cannot to do it justice here, but it does offer compelling observations about why we behave as we do in businesses. It also helps us understand why we accept invitations like those made by Jobs, Dyson, or the organizations they head.

Nearly all humans spend their lives in an uneasy relationship with power and authority. This stems from our formation in early years, where we grudgingly began to understand that the world wasn't simply there to gratify our needs for comfort, love and the occasional bite to eat. This process is a struggle, not least because we spend the first few months in a delicious paradise of having nearly all of our needs met on demand. Without any form of basic reasoning, a child has to develop ways of protecting itself against the strange and apparently random expectations of other human beings—and the intensity of emotion this brings on to the infant. (The child exists in a strange, mental world, to which our closest approximation may be the dream world we enter every night: a place where we experience ourselves both powerful and impotent, a circus characterized by hazardous and unexpected turns of events. As adults, when we awake, we struggle to make sense of these events. This is the permanent world of the one-year-old.)

In order to cope with the demands of the world, and our own responses to them, we develop certain defence strategies to protect us against feelings that threaten to overwhelm our young minds. These strategies may include the projection of bad feelings onto others, the denial of aggressive feelings or thoughts, or the warding off of a sense of hopelessness or paranoia. Because we intuit these feelings to be somehow illegitimate or abnormal, we push them underground, and our strategies against them become unknown to us. When we experience anxiety or stress, we often "regress" to these defence strategies. It's the most natural thing to do, since it's a pattern from our earliest years. This is why, for example, when you are angry, it is rarely for the reasons you think you are.

Work, as the authors Neumann, Kellner and Dawson-Shepherd point out, is an important counter-defensive behaviour, since it provides an opportunity for productive activity and growth.[34] Psychologically, however, there is something of a devil's bargain. In exchange for our energy and skills, we unconsciously ask the organization to respond exquisitely to our emotional requirements and needs. Oh yes, you do. It's the reason why we complain about our treatment, retail gossip and mull over supposed slights by our colleagues and managers. The feelings of injustice or anger may have legitimate causes, but they are largely to do with our own unwillingness to accept reality or responsibility for the place we find ourselves.

Why do we feel like this? It's because any organization is engaged in a primary task—its *raison d'être*. It could be saving lives in the casualty department of a hospital; or could be manufacturing small plastic dolls. The task demands that risks are taken and uncertainties are engaged in—risks and uncertainties that generate anxiety or stress. These anxieties invoke the defence routines we have discussed, setting up powerful cross-currents of emotion, of which the participants may or may not be aware. In any organization, one of the principal leadership tasks is to create a way in which the anxiety and energy of the workforce can be contained and channelled successfully.

Every place of work has to find ways to manage and contain these very human phenomena. Public-service organizations, for example, often have complex systems designed to ensure equitable treatment for illness, performance issues or grievances. They deal with anxiety bureaucratically.

When the primary task is framed in a narrative-rich and compelling fashion, and embodied by a charismatic leader, it can be deeply attractive. Do you want to come along and change the world, or what? The bargain with the charismatically-led business is a materially different one. The invitation is to join a cause. The implicit bargain is that you can lose some of yourself in this great adventure: that nagging sense of lack of direction or low self-worth will be quietened as you join the gang who are changing people's lives and kicking over conventional wisdom. Unlike most jobs, this is a release, not a constraint.

In psychodynamic terms, normal management provides an appropriate authority boundary around a task, to channel energy appropriately and manage anxiety. It's what managers are there for. (The demise of that much maligned species, the middle manager, has contributed greatly to the dramatic rise in reported workplace stress; there's no-one there any more to help contain the chatter.)

The charismatically-led business provides a slightly different sort of authority boundary—an ideology bound up with the actions of a heroic figure charting the course of the adventure. There is significant relief in investing your energy in these figures. Any effective leader is one who maintains a clear focus on and definition of the primary task. The effective charismatic does this by charging the task with a sense of momentum and momentousness. Characters like Dyson act as protagonists with whom large numbers of people can identify: they carry the burdens of hope and fear on behalf of their communities. They are constant, living embodiments of the primary task. In taking this role, they relieve people of significant—and rational—uncertainty, so that they can clear their minds and energy for the task.

The ego needs of the leader

In James Dyson's case, ego needs seem to be about the need to keep innovating, hence the disproportionate investment in research and development at Dyson. They are also about signalling to the world that success has been achieved. Consciously or unconsciously, the Dyson business is stacked with signals of distinctiveness. The headquarters is an icon, surrounded by iconic sculptures. The product is an icon. The founder is an icon. In an echo of his Victorian industrial forebears, Dyson has acquired an enormous country pile—Doddington Manor, in the south-west of England. When you are worth millions, is this just what you do, or is it a clear statement about joining the aristocracy on your own terms? And, as of 2007, he became Sir James Dyson, thereby becoming part of the official anti-establishment establishment along with Bob Geldof and Mick Jagger.

But back to business. What's it like when an ingenious, fully fledged charismatic is leading your organization? The answer is, in this case, largely beneficial.

A key benefit of Dyson's own personal drama, one suspects, is to help others engage in a rich sense of possibility. It's not too fanciful to suggest that he is recreating the conditions for others—particularly young designers and engineers—that he fought for, and revelled in, himself.

This helps us understand a lot of the genuine affection that exists within the business for this driven, quirky, jocular, demanding character. A story from his colleague, Alex Knox, helps capture this.

> **"It would have been about 2000 while we were tooling up for making the washing machine. The drum of the machine is a big component, so the machine that makes it is huge. So we're in this series of meetings with the contractors and James to sort out the issues, and one of the first is that the foundations of the factory aren't strong enough.**
>
> **James starts saying, 'I've been using this quick-drying cement at home—it's amazingly strong. If we fill it up we'll have some foundations.' So we did.**
>
> **The next problem was that the contractors couldn't get the machine**

through the door. James thinks for a while and suggests we could cut a hole in the wall. But we couldn't because of the building structure. Then he says we could take the roof panels off and use a big crane to drop it through. Then all the rain would get in, they said. So get a monster bit of tarpaulin . . . And it went on.

After all this, and after James had dismissed most of his own ideas as rubbish, we thought of a different way of sorting the problem." [35]

This story is of ingenuity and stubbornness, but the teller's enjoyment was in the way Dyson would openly and abruptly laugh at his own ideas. This is not a leader preoccupied with his own image as super-competent, as so many are. Indeed, the testimony of most is that Dyson ("James" to everyone) is very human. For most Dyson people, he is held in affection, not just esteem.

Charismatic leaders can come spectacularly unstuck in several ways. One is when their attention starts drifting from the primary task, a possibility given the restlessness of most entrepreneurs. The organization around them then starts to unravel, as people cease to be contained by the reassurance of the founder. But this hasn't happened. The main man is still focused. The ritual of making your own Dyson on your first day is there to tell you what the task is.

Another is when they fail to put in place sufficiently strong managers around them, because they fear constraints on their own actions. As we've seen, Dyson has been able to put in place a series of trusted lieutenants characterized by great competence and loyalty. This team, which is relatively young but long-serving, takes on the anxiety of the employees' principal questions, which could roughly be summarized as "What's James thinking?" and "What's James thinking about me/my project/my contribution?" This anxiety can, of course, spiral out of control. You can meet current or ex-Dyson people who loathe the man because they project a lot of their professional frustrations or need for recognition onto him.

People like Alex Knox, head of engineering and development for floor care, and Clare Mullin, group marketing director, have been with the Dyson business for nearly all their careers. Apart from their functional responsibilities, they act as interpreters of these questions.

In key areas, Dyson remains definitively present. Knox again:

> **"I think he really loves it [design and development]. He's so committed to it, all the way through. He spends a big chunk of his time down here . . . He enjoys getting involved in the nuts and bolts—and remains a really challenging person to work with."** [36]

However, he's inevitably grown more distant from the great majority of employees. That's why Knox, Mullin and people like them are needed—they're bridges. The organization devotes a great deal of time and attention to keeping information flowing and the Dyson ideology alive.

There is a studied informality of dress and contact, but there is also a well-choreographed process of employee communication, including monthly exchange sessions for all managers, café briefings for all employees, and a process called "my turn," where any employee can book a ten-minute slot with Martin McCourt to tackle a subject on their minds. In McCourt's words:

> **"One day, we'll break through one billion [UK pounds] . . . We'll get big and one of our challenges is to try and preserve the qualities that make it work here. If we can hang on to those, we can be whatever size we want."** [37]

One of those key qualities is the figure of Dyson himself. In a place that is tuned to the needs of the leader, it's difficult to imagine the course of the business if anything befell him. The very uniqueness of a charismatic leader can be the undoing of the place he leaves, voluntarily or involuntarily. Bill Critchley: "What if Dyson goes under a bus? This is purely speculative, but you imagine the place will gradually run down. These kinds of people are relied on for the energy and sexiness of an organization. It will make money, it will plod on . . . but will it maintain its dynamic?"

The Contrariness of the Contrarotator

Among the array of vacuum cleaners in the Dyson reception area stand two washing machines. They stand out because they are big and striking, and because Dyson doesn't, at the time of writing, actually sell washing machines. And therein lies a story.

The main function of money for the successful inventor–entrepreneur is to enable him or her to play some more. It would be no fun for James Dyson and the 300-strong research and development team simply to spend their time pushing the frontiers of the vacuum cleaner, although they continue to do that with vigour. There are new challenges out there. One of them is reinventing one of the world's key mechanical devices, as we'll see in the final chapter. Another is the way we wash our clothes.

This started by the simple observation of the way the vast majority of us do our laundry. We divide clothes into piles, each of which is valuable in different ways: a single load might have garments worth hundreds of pounds; the emotional value of different clothes to the wearer might be even more significant. We then put these piles into a mechanical drum, add in soap, chemicals and water, and press a button. The clothes then spend up to an hour alternately soaked and spun around in this mixture.

This sort of thing makes an engineer angry, in the same way that a clogging-up vacuum cleaner bag brings him out in a rash. It's so damned inefficient. There seem to be two main problems. First, if you sit and observe the cycle of your washing machine—and I challenge you to do so—you'll notice that the clothes spend a lot of time just sitting around in soiled, chemically charged water. Second, cleaning requires agitating the thing you are trying to clean. When you wash your hair, for example, you rub, use your fingers and use different angles of motion. You don't just smooth it in the same direction for ten minutes. Time and agitation. It could be a new school of philosophy: but Dyson had more practical things in mind.

The company spent a long time casting around for solutions. Steam and water-jet manipulation, microwave technology, hydro dynamics, ultrasound, vibration—even a rubber receptacle containing the clothes that was pummelled from the outside by hydraulic "fists." Over time, however, it focused on the insight that the most efficient method of cleaning clothes remains doing it by hand. In fact, 15 minutes washing by hand is as effective as four times as long in even an AAA rated machine. This is because we manipulate the garment more effectively, opening the weave of the fibre and giving more opportunity for the detergent to have its effect.

Now, just as with the development of the vacuum cleaner, we have poor performance of the existing machine, plus an insight into how it could be better. We then need a solution. For the cleaner, this was the application of cyclone technology. For the washing machine this was the application of two drums housed within the machine, operating in opposite directions: contra-rotation. In both cases, Dyson was creating a mechanical device that accelerated naturally occurring phenomena.

The Contrarotator Washing Machine

The emergent machine was appropriately mould-breaking. It made few concessions to the routine blandness of washing machine aesthetics and added significant additional capacity and innovative features to the basic contra-rotation message. The operating process was clear and intuitive. The machine tackled the long-standing problems of clogging conditioner drawers, radically improved the door seals, where you tend to get most leaks, used kink-free hoses and had a roller jack mechanism that ratcheted the machine onto wheels for ease of movement.

In 2001, the Contrarotator was launched in the UK. The approach was similar to the vacuum cleaner launches. Inventor is annoyed by basic inefficiency of a key domestic machine and disrupts conventional wisdom. The problem with all other machines in the category is that they don't work as well as they should. A new and strikingly designed species of the machine is produced. It becomes the most talked-about entrant for decades. It looked the business: the Dyson trademark muscularity, promising speed and no-nonsense performance.

It was a big bet for Dyson. This was the first significant new product launch, if we discount the robot vacuum, which was never a serious sales proposition. And, frankly, it was a big bet for a customer. The Contrarotator was eye-wateringly expensive. Here was a market with a £300–£500 modal price point, and Dyson was asking nigh on £1,000. Proportionally, it was a similar to the premium of the Dyson vacuum to the standard cleaner. In real terms, it was £500–£600. How much better is your washing going to be for that? In the words of an executive from one of the UK electrical-appliance retail chains:

"That's a big chunk of change to anybody, so you have to have a very convincing story. And it has to convince two people, because at that price, it's always a joint purchase between a husband and wife, or two partners. Also, you have the issue that you don't really have with vacuums which is that it's not just about the machine. People believe that the detergent and additives you use can make quite a difference to performance, so we suspect there were a lot of people thinking, well I'll just trade up to Ariel or Persil rather than trade up to this." [38]

Like the vacuum cleaner, the Contrarotator had to tackle the main category benefit head on. Remember that the positioning job with the cleaner was to persuade people of the virtues of not losing suction, which wasn't easy because flat out suction power was the market benchmark. This is why Dyson rarely claims superior suction—it sticks to better suction over a longer time. It has to choose its ground. With the washing machine, there was a similar quandary. It couldn't actually prove superior performance. What it could say was that you got great results in a much shorter time frame, because of the efficiency of the twin rotators imitating a good hand wash. There was a lot less pointless spinning around of wet clothes.

So Dyson, faced with the question, "Does it wash better, and at that price, twice as well?" could answer only equivocally. The claim was this: we believe it washes more clothes, very well, in a shorter time period, and with less damage. The less-damage-to-clothes claim makes intuitive sense at one level, since your beloved sweater spends less time soaking in phosphates, enzymes and the aggregate dirt of neighbouring underpants. At another, it doesn't, since by definition you are agitating the clothes more. I spoke to one of the technical directors at a leading detergent company, who said that their tests revealed that the machine "smacked the fibres about way too much for our liking." [39] (I love it when PhDs talk dirty). Dyson, of course, has a different point of view, and I'm not qualified to judge the merits of the different claims.

What we can piece together is this. The machine rapidly gained share in the premium sector of the UK market. There was a group of relatively price-insensitive customers, many of whom were owners of the company's vacuum cleaners. They traded up, and were broadly satisfied. But there wasn't the scale of purchase required, either to make it profitable for Dyson, or to satisfy the volume demands of the key electrical retailers that dominate the UK industry. The Contrarotator was withdrawn from sale in its only market, the UK, in early 2005.

A little digging reveals that there were two main reasons why sales weren't booming, and why word of mouth wasn't as effective as with the cleaner. The larger drum size (7kg, rather than the routine 4–5kg) was, intuitively, sensible. Who hasn't tried to stuff in more laundry and heave the door shut? Surely putting the machine on once every other day rather than daily is good news? But it had its flaws. There are three to four different sorts of "loads" for the average family: whites, coloureds, bedding/towels and more delicate items. Unless you have a gigantic washing/linen basket then you can't really store all these different loads until one of them is at a volume to justify a 7kg wash (apart from towels and bedding). You end up with a conflict between the routine washing behaviour and the demands of a bigger machine.

Another, and unexpected conflict with regular behaviour was that the promise of the fast wash wasn't really thought of as a benefit. Think about it. It's actually very rare that you're waiting for the machine to finish to grab that emergency piece of clothing. While a fast wash is more efficient in many ways, not least in energy use, we've trained ourselves into the expectation of an hour's cycle. We put the machine on, mentally note the time, and go away and get on with the other parts of life.

This meant that the crucial talk value of the machine was impaired. Nor was there the revelatory experience associated with your first Dyson vacuuming, when you fetched up for public display the hitherto invisible jetsam of your floors. As one consumer puts it:

> **"I remember using the washing machine for the first time, and it's great, don't get me wrong, but when I got out the clothes, they were, well, washed. There was none of that 'blimey' you got with the hoover. Sorry, the Dyson."** [40]
> Even fans occasionally struggle to escape the generic term.

So, despite its many advantages, the combination of cost and the stubbornness of existing laundry behaviour, meant the Contrarotator struggled for commercial traction. Some insiders at Dyson confess that, in retrospect, they got the balance wrong. The signals were there from the trade that the machine would struggle beyond a niche market. The premium was formidable. But, in the words of one, internally, "resistance was futile."

Strategically, it's important that Dyson stretches beyond the vacuum cleaner market. In its core market, there are no more big territories with well off consumers to conquer, although there's still a lot of share to grab. Cheaper and cheaper copies abound—you can buy something claiming to be a cyclone for £30 (50 euros) mail order. Beyond this is a nagging thought: "Will Dyson ever be anything more than the best vacuum cleaner company?" The ambition of the senior team is to replicate the magic—the reinvention of a core technology for a mass audience—elsewhere.*

With the washing machine, there is the promise that there will be some form of relaunch. The betting is that this will be a similar, but cheaper machine, targeted at the US market. The Contrarotator will live to fight another day. It's too good a machine not to.

---

* As this book was being finalized, Dyson launched the Airblade, a hand dryer designed for public bathrooms and hotels, service stations, pubs, hospitals and schools. It cuts the average hand-drying time from 30 seconds to 10 seconds and uses 20 percent of the power, while cunningly taking the Dyson brand name out of the home and into the public domain.

Chapter 8
Marketing: The Dyson Way

"I want a Dyson, so, so bad. I lust for the Dyson . . . I am so going to get a Dyson"

Posted on April 5, 2005 on US consumer blog

> **"I don't think of us as a brand at all.
> I believe they've developed branding
> as a way to mask the fact that their
> product isn't any different."** [41]
> James Dyson, interview, November 2005

In the opening chapter, we touched on Dyson's insistence that they aren't really a brand. Being tarred with the flimflammery of marketing disturbs them at several levels.

When I put this to marketing professionals, they are predictably sceptical. Come on, they say. If it's just about the product, why is it purple and lime? Why do they place such importance on the man's story? Why do they pay so much attention to after care, even putting the helpline number on the product? Why are you writing a book about it?

This tension has nagged away at me throughout the writing. And I think it needs closer exploration.

What Dyson thinks about branding

James Dyson believes that "branding" is about disguising yourself. That it's an attempt to conceal the fact that:

a your product is no different from anything else;

b you are no different either.

I suspect this stems from the "purity of solution" school. A man in a lab coat stands before you. This device/tool/drug/code has been engineered perfectly and tested to destruction. It's the best in the world at dealing with this problem. All we need to do is put it in people's hands, and they'll put their hands in their pockets.

This is why many engineers and designers despise marketing. They experience it as a muffler, placing barriers between customers and the solution.[42] Cleverness supersedes the simplicity of the approach.

Then we have to remember the Dyson world view of conventional industry, particularly its own. It's a world of chicanery, where second best is good enough and where product claims never match the experience. Marketing is a travelling fair, a theatre show where customers are deluded into parting money with ineffective goods that trade on the basis of unearned reputation. You dupe others and discount yourself. Roll up, roll up.

What marketers mean by branding
Branding, at its most basic level is a way of conferring ownership. You brand cattle with the name or symbol of your farm so no-one else can claim them. You name your product after yourself. Dyson, for example.

At the next level, you find yourself in a market for products. Other people are competing for your trade, for your livelihood. To guard against this, you need to confer identity. You give people a set of stimuli to remind them with whom they are dealing: a sign or icon; a distinctive method of packing, labelling or transporting the product. These are pegs that allow busy people to hang associations onto you. You design your product differently to show its features. You use advertising to point out your advantages.

At the third level, having survived the market for products, you are in a market for meaning. To thrive here, you confer meaning by making your product part of a larger story. You sponsor or fund complementary activities. You persistently communicate your origin and cause, placing yourself within a larger narrative of purpose. You merchandise the intent of the business: for example, to create cleaner, better homes; to encourage inventiveness and progress; to reward and recognize unsung professions and professionals.

What they can learn from each other

Dyson, therefore, does instinctively what a great brand professional would advise it to do. That is: design an outstandingly competitive and interesting product, make your own beliefs transparent and part of the selling story, and place yourself in a different category of meaning from your competition.

But this is where branding theory and practice fracture. There are very few of these great brand professionals around. Real branding is about origin, or it is nothing. It is not about what you should do because market research tells you so. It is what you have to do. Only that belief will sustain you through the assault course of starting and growing a business.

The world of branding has a million practitioners ready to assist and advise you. It is a land of consultants, researchers, designers, writers, account managers, linguists and academics. They have one thing in common. With a few graceful exceptions, they know nothing about you: they can't. They can only know you through the filter of what they want to sell you. A researcher sees the opportunity for more insight; a designer sees new corporate literature. An advertising agency will rarely say, "Don't think you've got the product right. We'll come back when you're ready."

The co-author of *The Cluetrain Manifesto*, Doc Searls, puts its like this:

"Where does your company come from? Where do you come from? What is your truth?
Those are the real questions you should start by asking. Those are the questions you should start answering. If you aren't answering them already. Positioning is a matter of getting honest and real with yourselves and your customers. You can't job it out." [43]

Dyson is rightly contemptuous of people who want to brand it. Because branding can't be "jobbed out"; only you can brand you. Only you can know what you really are, if you're willing to do the work and find out.

If you've spent rather too much of your life, as I have, in conversations about brand image, positioning, equity and models, this approach is a tonic. Two colleagues of mine recall the takeover of their design agency by one of the big brand consulting companies. In an attempt to help everyone understand each other, a dictionary of terms was produced. "'A' had a few items and then 'B' had about 30, brand attributes, brand distinctions, brand this, brand that. You kind of gave up at that point." There is a lot of jaw-dropping nonsense about brands spoken by apparently intelligent and well-meaning people.

Let us be clear. You still need branding people, unless you're planning to write every brochure, code every website and run every survey yourself. But they can't tell you who or what you are and what you must project. Only you can.

Is there anything in the Dyson-esque belief that branding is a camouflage job, concealing flaws and so-so product? Frankly, yes, even though its position is a little rhetorical.

There is very little that is distinctive. We saw in Chapter 6 how hard it is for start-up businesses, in the face of rather conservative markets and bankers, to launch anything different. The fall back position is that if it were really an opportunity, we'd have seen it out there or done it ourselves. Within big companies, radical proposals tend to get sidelined, as their payback is uncertain and they might eat into sales of existing lines. And why invest anyway? The idea would get reverse-engineered and be on the market within months as a copy. Big organizations become, despite their protestations, innovation-free zones. Nothing can evolve because there's no allowance for mutation.

Professional branding has developed as a set of techniques to encourage you to look beyond a product's more obvious characteristics and to train you to associate a set of meanings or feelings with the aforesaid product. (Or, depending on your point of view, as a sort of Zimmer frame for products that can't quite stand up on their own.) Persil? You're a good Mum. Citibank? You know your finances. Nike? You take no quarter. Marketers and advertisers do this partly because it's good fun, but mostly because it makes more money. A brand is a product or service backed by a level of customer belief. That belief means a good stream of revenue.

Professor Peter Doyle, the sadly deceased doyen of professional marketing, described a successful brand (S) as the combination of an effective product (P), a distinctive identity (D) and added values (AV) by which he means the feelings (F) that the brand elicits.

This is the sort of seductive algorithm beloved by the technically minded brand professional, but it's useful here to make a point.

I think there is a distinction between the Dyson/Searls' approach to life and that of the contemporary branding industry. The latter spends a lot of time on (F)—emoting. Often faced with indifferent or only marginally superior product performance, it spends alarming amounts of money and resources trying to understand what feelings products should be eliciting. The marketers then embark upon tortuous design and advertising paths to work out ways of doing this. They target our emotions in order to manipulate them. Often, we lap this up, and knowingly. It's a game we play.

Inanimate object
> Hey, I'm not a bottle of hair detergent, I'm several orgasms in a shower.

Shopper
> You're naughty, but I like you.

Scanner
> Beep!

This is not just strange behaviour, says the Dyson school of marketing. It's illegitimate. You're pretending. You're concealing the fact that you're very ordinary by dressing up as something more interesting. You're like all those vacuum cleaner manufacturers who fibbed for years.

If we put the semantics in their place, we get something like this. By any decent definition, Dyson is a brand. It's a product whose meaning is actively and successfully managed. But acting as if you aren't a brand is liberating. It means you don't get caught in endless rounds of second guessing of competitors and consumer research. You get out and play your own game, rather than watching videos of the opposing team's last match. You follow your convictions. For the technically minded—make your P the best in the world, be resolute about D and let F follow.

Dyson has astutely recognized that the currency of branding has become corrupted.

"I've issued a fatwa against the word brand round here," the group marketing director, Clare Mullin, says gleefully. It's become a barrier to doing things, she explains: you only have to say the word and people assume you're engaged in some form of manipulation or swagger. Mullin, like many others, has given up using the word, because it has become culturally debased. Soon, "brand" will be the equivalent of "USP" or "punter"—nouns that used to be common to business conversations, but are now only uttered by the fatally misinformed. Films such as *The Corporation*, *Super Size Me*, and the recent *Wal-Mart: The High Cost of Low Price* are far more effective at recasting the characters of corporations than the remonstrances of the marketing or branding community will ever be.

The key features of a marketing strategy where The Brand loses its self-importance are as follows.

Number 1
The product's in charge

> **"The answer is always the product."**
> Clare Mullin

Because marketers tend to be at the faster-moving and snazzy end of the business, they sometimes get carried away. Often encouraged by people from Brandland they dwell in a sort of parallel universe of focus groups and workshops where people are consumers, selling is campaigning and intangibility is the new rock and roll.

Not at Dyson. This is why the most important thing a new employee does on their first day is to strip and reassemble a Dyson vacuum cleaner. Some see this as the charming quirk of a product-focused business. It is not. It is a ritual designed to ensure that you never get above yourself. You're here because of the machine and you're here for the machine. It's not quite a marine and his rifle, but it's not far off.

If you believe your product is thumpingly superior, it makes your life a lot easier as a marketer. If you read any of the marketing business publications, you'll find numerous executives being quoted on their brand's launch activity, campaign or product variation. They will talk—alas, rarely convincingly—about showcasing the brand's qualities, raising awareness or extending consumer choice. They tend not to press-release statements such as:

**"This is a nakedly superior product
and we want the world to know."**

Marketers rarely get to take refuge in the engineer's testable assertions that this is better than that, end of story. So they love it when they can say things like "the vast majority of vacuum cleaners/products in this category don't work properly: this one does" and get away with it. You don't get to do that in most other markets.

The other great advantage of a superior product is that you can cloak yourself in naivety to retailer, journalist and consumer alike. I'm not trying to sell you this, you say. Take one, try it, and see for yourself. Which is a rather clever way of engaging their interest. Over time, this naivety has become as cleverly engineered as the brush beater in the DC08.

There is one important take on this approach, however. Only claim superiority on the ground you choose. For Dyson, this is "no loss of suction." You can't say "better suction," because that's not strictly true. You say better suction over a longer period of time. There are other products with better suction and more powerful motors, even though their performance tails off. Nor can you stake great claims for reliability. Which?, the UK's leading consumer testing organization, had poor things to say about Dyson's reliability in its 2005 report.[44] Bottom of the pile in fact. So choose your ground.

**Number 2
A killer experience**

The writer and marketing authority John Grant speaks persuasively of businesses that manage to get up close and personal: they move from the realm of the objective and formal to the subjective and intimate in their approach.[45] Mostly this is done through communications, but also through services and experiences that encircle or seduce you. The Nike 10K speaks to you not as athlete, but as runner-as-human-being. Docusoaps and reality TV busily deconstruct our assumptions about behaviour in the public and private realms.

After the development of the cyclone, the single greatest piece of brilliance from Dyson was the transparent housing of the machine. When you first use your Dyson, you see all the shit you've been living in. It may well be that another new vacuum cleaner with a bag would have picked up similar amounts of stuff. But you wouldn't have seen it, except when you emptied the bag over a dustbin, and even then your eyes would probably have been averted. (Even, now, many of the manufacturers can't quite bring themselves to do this. My Electrolux Cyclonic has a sort of smoked grey housing. The design team is saying, "You don't really want to look in there, do you?")

But there it is. The dust. The stray bits of fibre. The alien, indefinable items that you don't really want to investigate. Dyson contact centre employees will excitedly tell you about the emails, letters and calls they receive on the theme of "You Wouldn't Believe It." The cat hair from the animal that died ten years ago. Pieces of fibre from clothing worn by the people who used to live in the house. The tearful mother as she stares at the collected dust from the bedroom of her asthmatic child.

The move into the US has elicited ever more hysterical confessions of "What Lies Beneath" the carpets of everyday American homes. This is the land where the lust for transformative domestic experiences knows no bounds. I gotta tell you this has changed my life.

This initial experience of dishing the dirt is fundamental to the product's success. Anthropologists call it an acquisition ritual. It's an important part of taking ownership of an object, of making it part of your life and is often associated with the first use of the object. First the Walkman, then the iPod made music your own. This makes your dirt your own.

The experience is an important step on from the old Hoover demonstrator, who would shake out soil onto the store carpet and remove it. But now this isn't anyone else's soil, madam, it's yours.

These are excerpts from conversations with ordinary owners during the research for this book.

"Well, I filled it up from downstairs and then again from upstairs. Then another half from downstairs. I was gobsmacked."

"My husband went around for an hour and every so often made me look at it. Look, he said, look at that stuff. He loved it, so he did."

"I rang my sister to get her to come over and see. She took one look then nicked it for a day. She didn't want to give it back either."

"I just couldn't believe we'd been living in that filth, it was really upsetting. I waited till my husband came home and I said, 'Look, look at what we've been living in.'"

"There was a lot of muck in there, though I'm not sure if that was the Dyson or the fact that we hadn't done much hoovering before!" [46]

This is Operation Shock and Awe. The shock is the sight, which is accompanied by strong pangs of wonder or guilt, depending on your disposition or upbringing. The awe is of the growing, spinning piles of detritus, an awe that is projected onto the machine. It is a strong confirmation of purchase. If you've paid premium dollars/euros/yen for this, you want it to be awesome.

Crucial, too, is the social function of the ritual. Unless you're deeply embarrassed by your own hygiene standards, you want to show other people. People show their partners. They confront their children with the evidence embedded in their bedroom carpets. They show their neighbours or friends. The display has a strange sense of celebration about it; a constraint has been released, a wrong righted.

The cleansing ritual goes deep into all cultures and resonates through history. The recently elected President Morales of Bolivia went through such a ritual upon assuming office in 2006. The African belief in foot track magic, where evil spirits would enter through your feet, demanded a routine cleansing of the environment. Jewish, Islamic and Zoroastrian cultures have purifying and cleaning rituals. There is clearly practical advantage in cleanliness, to ward off disease and bacteria. But in cleaning our bodies and our homes, we also are symbolically renewing ourselves, making ourselves whole. If you don't believe me, think about how you have a bath: how you prepare yourself, what you put in, how you pace or relax yourself, how you dry and anoint your body: how you feel different.

And so with your carpet or floor. The initial drawing out of dirt sets a pattern of cathartic gratification. It's the killer experience.

Number 3
Earn your stripes

The Dyson launch strategy in different countries is marked by an inversion of the normal practice of highly supported campaigns and national coverage. In a pattern started in the UK and Australia, you have to put in an enormous amount of ground work and seeding to earn early distribution and sales. This qualifies you for advertising and promotional support from the mother ship. Culturally, this is to reinforce the founder experience: use your ingenuity and faith in the product to get a foothold in the market, and you'll really know what Dyson is all about. Financially, it means you're not substantially exposed in the first year or so.

It's an approach that finds favour with other brands that challenge the status quo on limited resources.

> **"Advertising is the last thing you bring to the mix. You start by getting your product right, your attitude right, getting everyone internally understanding the mission. Then you move to telling the story through PR. You build the advertising last and that way you can live off realistic budgets."** [47]
> Amy Curtis-McIntyre of JetBlue Airways (quoted in *The Pirate Inside* by Adam Morgan)

Many of the challenger brands that Adam Morgan describes in *The Pirate Inside* act like missionaries. They are fired by zeal for their beliefs, have few resources and therefore have to improvise at every turn. The native people are indifferent, or if roused, can be hostile, bringing to bear the weight of tradition and convention on your fragile expeditionary force.

An example. In Belgium, in the mid-to-late 1990s, Dyson was beginning to establish itself and felt confident enough to invest in a little press advertising. Its approach was the usual refrain: your current cleaner loses suction, so this lot (cue pile of detritus) remains in your carpet. With a Dyson, it won't.

In a delicious irony, Belgium, at the heart of the trade-liberalizing, cartel-busting European community, prohibited comparative advertising. A test for the missionaries. They decided to place the ad, judging that the rumpus would earn them much more publicity than a couple of press ads ever would. And they were right. A trade organization of six vacuum cleaner manufacturers took out an injunction against them. In doing so, of course, they walked into the intended David versus Goliath narrative trap laid for them. Dyson could play the plucky outsider merely trying to offer relief to the beleaguered and dusty Belgian citizen.

The game played out. The courts were obliged to place restraints on Dyson, and ordered it to remove any offending images or text implying directly superior performance. Rather than sit back and lick its wounds, Dyson gleefully complied, sticking pieces of black tape over every box of product and piece of literature that was bound for Belgium. Each piece of tape was the stimulus for a conversation with a journalist, a retailer or a potential customer. "Why have you blacked out this picture with tape?" "I'm really sorry, I can't tell you, because my competitors have taken me to court." The kind of interest and intrigue advertisers can only dream of was immediately created.

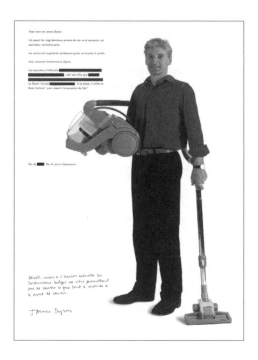

Note, however, that the decision to do this was about earning stripes. Do we have the courage to do this? Do we really want to stick one up the European Commission? Annoy important people in a growing market? Stick thousands of bits of black tape onto brochures? Yes. Sure we do.

Number 4
People the brand

Connecting the brand with the people behind it endows it with the quality of a story. A product without a narrative is a sorry thing. If you can connect, you achieve something spectacular: you make the business human. This is an advantage with which a large organization cannot compete. Unilever paid hundreds of millions of dollars for Ben & Jerry's because it saw a humanity they didn't have and couldn't invent. Likewise L'Oréal with its purchase of The Body Shop.

It helps, of course, to have a charismatic and articulate founder to tell your origin myth. (Another lovely example is Gert "Ma" Boyle, the 80-year-old matriarch who's still chairman of the board at Columbia Sportswear). But there are many other ways to do it. You describe the way that people invented or stumbled upon the product you're enjoying right now, as Nike has done with Bill Bowerman and Jeff Johnson, two of its early wizards. You tell the story of the ordinary people of the business going about their job, doing extraordinarily ordinary things. You describe the way customers or communities have been touched or transformed by contact with you.

One of my own clients is Caledonian Breweries in Edinburgh. Go to *www.caledonian-brewery.co.uk*, and you'll find not the usual executive profiles, but virtually everyone who works there, as defined by their upbringing, favourite pin-up, pub and their last purchase over £300. It's completely in tune with individual beers brought to you by individuals. It's what Starbucks attempts to do with the little profiles of the barista and their favourite drink. Alas the "favourite" is invariably the quintuple latte eggnog ginger latte costing you half your weekly outgoings.

A slightly better example are the book recommendations from booksellers at Waterstone's or Barnes & Noble that adorn every other shelf.

You attach interest and accessibility to your brand by letting your audience know that you are human beings, rather than executives, and serve people rather than consumers. You have joys, enthusiasms and hang ups like the rest of us.

Number 5
Word of mouth

Building on work by Roger Fidler, John Grant explains that there are three fundamental media that humans use to communicate with one another. One is display—TV advertising, painting, photography. Another is writing. The third is conversation.

What marketing needs to find is ways to fuel word of mouth recommendations as richly, humanely and evocatively as display advertising-fuelled metaphorical added values. [48]

No advertising can be as effective as someone you know recommending use. In the 1990s in the UK, this was literal word of mouth. In the noughties, it can be boosted by electronic word of mouth. Here are excerpts from a US consumer website. Forget all the marketing plans: this is marketing in action. [49]

....
@ 12:06 (PST) on December 7, 2004

> We're moving to a place with carpets, so . . . we're going to need a vacuum. I keep seeing this Dyson dude on the tube, telling me that my current vacuum isn't a Dyson. I don't even know what kind of model we've got, but it doesn't work well. Do I do the Dyson thing and be all trendy? Is this guy full of nothing

but hot, recycled air? Should I get the low reach or the animal upright? Its yellow shell is a little off-putting, but not if this sucker really doesn't suck at sucking. When vacuums lose suction, you replace the bag. When a Dyson loses suction, it's gotta be broken.

Re: The Dyson Vacuum

I bought one about a month ago . . . and dang. Hoover ain't got nothin on it. Not that I'm all geeky about my vacuum cleaner, but it works really well. I have two chocolate labs, and they shed like crazy in the fall. Normally it's a pain to keep what little carpet I do have clean. I recommend it.

Re: The Dyson Vacuum

I've had a Dyson machine for nearly a year now (DC11 model) and it's simply superb. When I first got it, I did a test, I vacuumed my house with my old machine, then immediately did the same with the Dyson—and it filled the bin—that's after the carpets were allegedly "cleaned" by my old machine!

As you've got pets, I'd recommend going for a model with the "turbobrush" as it'll be much better for getting the hairs up, and the brush is easy to dismantle and clean out should it get clogged.

Re: The Dyson Vacuum by Steve Butler at 12:53 (PST) on Dec 7, 2004

The first time we bought one (a DC01) back in England it filled the dust container in just 2 rooms!

You'll wonder what your old vacuum did—I'm sure all its predecessor did was redistribute the dirt. When we moved to here in the US in 2002 we were lucky enough to trackdown the distributor's number on the web. (They weren't yet sold in stores).

Don't hoover the floor, Dyson it—you'll never regret it

....

Re: The Dyson Vacuum by Anonymous at 02:41AM (PST) on Dec 8, 2004

My mother's had one for two or three years. Every visit she takes ten minutes to tell me how good it is. I've never heard a bad word about them.

....

Re: The Dyson Vacuum by bnaivar at 03:56AM (PST) on Dec 8, 2004

NO, No, No!!!!! My wife works at a sewing machine and vacuum store. They all say that Dyson is a piece of crap! It also costs more to fix than replace.

....

Re: The Dyson Vacuum by Anonymous at 05:40AM (PST) on Dec 8, 2004

Had a Dirt Devil, and got an Orek for present. We inherited a Dyson and DANG! If there was EVER a vac to be geeky about—it's a Dyson.

Yes, we vacuumed with the DD and then the Orek. The Orek picked up stuff the DD didn't (no surprise there). The Dyson picked up stuff I swear was in the carpet from 1975! You must possess a Dyson.

Re: Re: Re: The Dyson Vacuum by Anonymous at 10:30AM (PDT) on Jun 23, 2005

Well, we purchased a Dyson because we bought into all the marketing hype, and it turned out that it was in fact a very powerful sucking machine. The problem is, it broke after less than 3 months. So we take it back to Target and we get a replacement, no problem, we must have gotten a lemon, right?

Well, less than 3 months later, once again, the vacuum has completely lost suction. I thought the guy said "It won't lose suction. Ever." It's all lies. The Dyson is an all-plastic piece of shit. Sure, it's powerful, when it works, but it is not reliable. I don't know what vacuum we're going to get now, but we won't be getting another Dyson.

Re: The Dyson Vacuum by Anonymous at 01:57PM (PST) on Mar 20, 2005

Well I just bought a dyson dc08 twin cylinder animal version today and oh blimey!!! I decided to have a go at the zorb powder—the guy at the shop said he just sprinkles it on and it does the trick. ALL I can say is I am absolutely shocked I mean really shocked at how much stuff this thing picks up!!!!!! 2 and 3/4 full after the first go and I mean I live in a small flat! I have 2 cats and to be honest I felt quite sick seeing all this stuff whisking around lots of hair and loads of white stuff (not the zorb powder, this is after

I had done that bit). I thought the two turbine heads were great, I used the smaller with my hand, I was really surprised by how good it is a doing the edges.

....

Re: The Dyson Vacuum by Anonymous at 09:21AM (PST) on Mar 26

It's kinda like the vacuum cleaner version of a Ferrari; it's a status symbol, cute as hell, high tech, fun, noisy, expensive, a bit fragile; and neither the fastest vacuum available nor the best. But it still works really quite well, and it's a long, long way from being the worst. Bags are a nuisance and fiddly.

And if you're like me, you just *want* one.

....

Re: Re: The Dyson Vacuum by Anonymous at 07:00PM (PDT) on May 12, 2005

I worked for Sears Roebuck and Co for 4 years in division 20. Sears lingo for the carpet cleaning department.

I have seen machines come and go, but I have to say the Dyson is probably in the top 3 that I have seen. Eurekas are crap. Kenmore or Dyson are your best bet. Followed by Hoover. Hoover has the design problem of having the fan in the dirt path. So all the stuff you vac up runs through the fan and can make it lose suction over time due to the fan getting chipped away, gummed up.

There are 50 entries, and around 45 are positively disposed to Dyson, including the lustful drive-by shopper who opened the chapter.

Word of mouth recommendations give you enhanced legitimacy. They're another manifestation of a more human approach to marketing, since you let fellow human beings do the work for you. They create confidence on your behalf, and this can blossom remarkably quickly.

The phenomenon requires certain conditions.

First, a fertile environment in which news spreads quickly. The most obvious example is an equity or commodity market. A rumour starts about a new stock, positive or negative. The market is sensitive to such news and responds by buying and selling. Momentum develops, until the system reestablishes itself at a different equilibrium.

With word of mouth the initial currency is not money but an idea about how things could be different, in a way relevant to the people in a particular environment. This idea is in competition with others, and it is selected for interest and fitness.

A whole field called memetics studies the phenomenon, and the best place to start is Susan Blackmore's *The Meme Machine*.[50] The radical implication of the field is that our brains are at the behest of competing memes (imitable bits of ideas, language or imagery) in the same way that our bodies are simply means for our genes to have their way. That's a philosophical step too far for this book, but it helps explain word of mouth, and, specifically, Dyson's success.

The fertile environment in Dyson's case is that of house and home conversations. It's a very rich area, and one that marketers spend billions of pounds trying to inveigle their way into. Companies like Procter & Gamble and Ikea have made fortunes by influencing these conversations. The exchanges happen over coffee in someone's house, walking home from dropping off the children at school, at informal family gatherings. They're often between women, but not necessarily. "Have you tried X?" "Do you know a decorator?" "They've sold that house down the road, you know." "Did you see X?"

To prosper in this environment, you need elements of relevant difference, so that conversations can attach themselves. The core elements of difference are these:

1 **The product aesthetic: it looks different.**
   This doesn't have to be radical. Simple, small things can provoke conversation. Toothpaste that comes out of a pump, rather than a tube; bath salts that come in a little "bomb" ready to drop.

2 **The product effect: it works differently.**
   If you're Dyson, you have a killer experience (see above). But equally, the bath salts fizzle, or the work top comes up cleaner.

3 **The product or brand narrative: it has a human reason for being this way.**
   Someone thought it would be fun. Someone thought it would be important. Someone put themselves in jeopardy in order to get it here.

And the better these three support one another, the better the conversation.

So, were Dyson to publish its *Guide to Marketing*, it would probably look something like the following:

dyson

Number 1
The product's in charge

You can play marketing games to your heart's content, but if you don't know and believe you have something better to offer, you'll always be hobbled. You'll be faking it.

Number 2
A killer experience

A tangible expression of your product's effectiveness, delivered against a major customer concern is priceless.

Number 3
Earn your stripes

Faith is required, as are courage and chutzpah. If you can survive in the crucible of low resources and big obstacles, you qualify for success.

dyson

Number 4
People the brand

Allow the brand to take on human qualities
by making it clear how those in the business
"author" it for your benefit and their own
fulfilment.

Number 5
Word of mouth

If you want word of mouth (and who
doesn't?), ensure you have the ingredients
of relevant difference that will prompt
interesting conversations.

Coda
A Life Less Ordinary

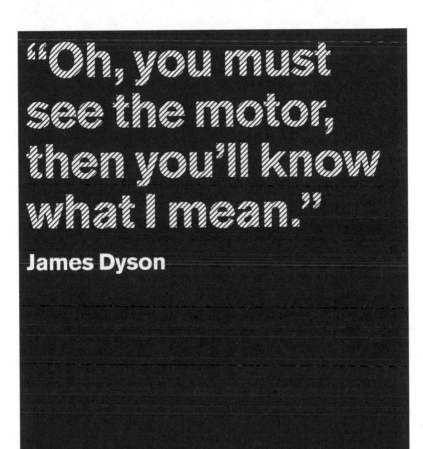

"Oh, you must see the motor, then you'll know what I mean."

James Dyson

Dyson HQ

I'm sitting outside James Dyson's office, waiting to be ushered in. The relaxed intensity and chumminess of my visit begins to subside. This is open plan, but I'm in an antechamber. My host gets slightly nervous, managing herself as we approach the appointment time. I'm nervous now. It flicks through my mind that there is a category of organizational story called "Face to Face With God." I recall Joel Bakan's account of interviewing the economist Milton Friedman, when Friedman's assistant warned him that if his subject found the questions "boring," he'd probably walk out. I shift in my seat. Dyson's PA sits at a desk outside the corner suite, a sentinel. The public relations team is the closest working group to his office, and I imagine the burden of being the people most in view of the founder. Probably keeps you on your toes.

I'm led in. Dyson himself is articulate, charming and very practised. He's been interviewed a million times before. The conversation isn't, somehow, what I'd hoped. He listens carefully to my questions, clarifying what they mean before answering. He moves smoothly into narratives of the cleaner, innovation, the nature of the company. I know all this, I'm thinking. I'm beginning to panic that I probably have one chance with the guy and I'm not getting anything but the gloss.

We're talking about invention and the process of iterative testing and the accepting of constant failure as you develop new ideas. Then:

> **"Have you seen the motor?"**
> **"No."**
> **"Oh, you must see the motor, then you'll know what I mean. I've got it in the back of the car. Can we get the motor in so he can see?"**

A black case is brought in about a minute later.

> **"The electric motor in our vacuum cleaners really annoyed me, so we've built a better one."**

And he's off.

I'm someone whose last encounter with electric motors was memorizing a diagram of the DC version for my physics O level. Without any understanding of what it was or how it was meant to work, I just scraped a pass. But I'm glued.

> **"This is a regular motor, which has lots of problems . . . one of which is that these carbon brushes wear out, and they run on the commutator, which is that copper thing. These copper strips here are, amazingly, glued on . . . and they fall off . . . each one of those has to be in phase for the next one . . . and each one of those wires has to be insulated and measured. Burn out is caused by break down of insulation . . . and this is limited to 30,000rpm, which means you have to have a relatively big motor to achieve the power you want and the air flow you want . . ."**

The narrative turns out to be brilliant in its simplicity. Electric motors have been much the same since Faraday, they've got loads of faults, so we've built a better one. (Heard the one about vacuum cleaners?) The motivation is that "it really annoyed me" and that everyone else seemed to accept the situation . . .

"So we've developed a completely different kind of motor which is less than half the weight of that, has 40 percent more power and never wears out . . . It goes at 110,000rpm."

He contrasts one metal object with another, smaller, shinier one. Technically, I don't have a clue what's going on, but I know it's something significant.

During this, James Dyson takes on a different energy. He doesn't have to rehearse the vacuum story any more, well though he does it. He's got in his hands something that has fascinated and captivated him and his R&D team, and now it's up and running. He's not doing PR for a book, he's explaining how a machine works and why it could change the landscape for ever. This is the man who clambered over a saw mill at night doing sketches.

It's enchanting, and I use the word in its original sense of saying an incantation, of casting a spell. Here is that precise combination of effort, curiosity and revelation that powered the original story. And if the thing is as good as he says it is, which I have no way of judging, then it's bigger than the cleaner. A small share of the electric motor market is a lot bigger than a large share of the vacuum cleaner market.

The other thing to note is that the investment and development of the motor would simply not have happened in the ordinary corporate environment.

Someone in the bowels of Ford or Electrolux has been down this way, tinkering, imagining. "What if we built a much better electric motor?" They may even have a project going. Then someone slaps them down or pats them on the head and says, "We can't take it any further, and you know, we're not really in the electric motor market anyway. I'm sure GE or Hitachi are on to this."

Off into the November night, through Wiltshire roads to Chippenham station. On the way home to London, I hold the image of the motor in my mind, and think of the energy of human endeavour. It seems appropriate that James Dyson invents things that spin very, very fast, be they cleaners or motors, and go doing so in perpetuity. The Dyson business itself spins fast: the sense of productive turmoil is palpable. The whole place is precious, but quite fragile, someone senior told me in an unguarded moment.

The maelstrom of activity is contained now, tied to the floor in a way it wasn't some years ago. But the energy and pace are signatures of the founder.

It's the positive side of anxiety, says a reflective former employee I speak to that evening. James's restless anxiety to pioneer and push beyond the commonplace are enthralling, he says, and you've just been enthralled.

> **"The experience of working there is to sense your part in that movement. He triggers that in others, and they channel their own energy into his uber-project. It can feel wonderful."**

And that's the offer of both the company and the brand: a life less ordinary.

Endnotes

1   Transactions of the Newcomen Society, 1934-35, http://www.newcomen.com/excerpts/vacuum_cleaner/index.htm

2   http://www.sciencemuseum.org.uk/on-line/vacuums/didyouknow.asp

3   Justin Cartwright, *The Promise of Happiness* (Bloomsbury, 2004)

4   Interview, November 2005

5   *How I Made It: 40 successful entrepreneurs reveal all*, Rachel Bridge (Kogan Page 2005)

6   Interview, November 2005

7   http://www.wfs.org/tabeles.htm

8   Interview, December 2005

9   *Focus on Health and Safety*, Trades Union Congress, London (December, 2000)

10   Shoshana Zuboff and James Maxmin, *The Support Economy: Why corporations are failing individuals and the next episode of capitalism* (Penguin, 2004)

11   Interview, January 2005. Mickey wanted to say that he's never been in a footnote before.

12   Interviews, October 2005

13   www.bbc.co.uk

14   James Dyson, *Against The Odds: An autobiography* (Texere, 2000)

15   ibid

16   ibid

17   Interview, January 2006

18   Joel Bakan, *The Corporation: The pathological pursuit of profit and power* (Constable & Robinson, 2005)

19   Dyson, op. cit.

20   Joseph Campbell, *The Hero With A Thousand Faces* (Paladin, 1993)

21   Christopher Vogler, *The Writer's Journey: Mythic Structure for Writers* (Pan, 1999)

22   http://www.chamberonline.co.uk/YTOi-wNoHMvRUA.html

23 Michael E. Gerber, *The E Myth Revisited: Why most small businesses don't work and what to do about it* (HarperCollins, 1994)

24 Dyson, op. cit.

25 Correspondence, February 2006

26 Interview, February 2006

27 Interview, November 2005

28 Interview, November 2005

29 Interview, November 2005

30 Correspondence, March 2006

31 *Guardian*, February 6, 2002

32 http://jeremy.zawodny.com/blog/

33 Interview, January 2006

34 J. Neumann, K. Kellner and A. Dawson-Shepherd, *Developing Organizational Consultancy* (Routledge, 1997)

35 Interview, November 2005

36 Interview, November 2005

37 Interview, November 2005

38 Interview, February 2006

39 Interview, February 2006

40 Interview, January 2006

41 Interview, November 2005

42 Thanks to Russell Davies for this point.

43 Rick Levine, Christopher Locke, Doc Searls and David Weinberger, *The Cluetrain Manifesto* (FT.COM, 2000)

44 http://www.which.co.uk/reports_and_campaigns/house_and_home/Reports/cleaning/

45 John Grant, *The New Marketing Manifesto: The 12 rules for building successful brands in the 21st century* (Texere, 2000)

46 Customer conversations, January 2006

47 Grant, op. cit.

48 ibid

49 http://www.hipfamily.com/archives/2005/04/vacuum_cleaners.html

50 Susan Blackmore, *The Meme Machine* (Oxford University Press, 2000)

Bibliography

Joel Bakan, *The Corporation: The pathological pursuit of profit and power* (Constable & Robinson, 2005)

Gregory Bateson, *Steps to an Ecology of Mind: Collected essays in anthropology, psychiatry, evolution and epistemology* (University of Chicago Press, 2000)

Susan Blackmore, *The Meme Machine* (Oxford University Press, 2000)

Christopher Booker, *The Seven Basic Plots: Why we tell stories* (Continuum, 2004)

Joseph Campbell, *The Hero With A Thousand Faces* (Paladin, 1993)

Ernest Dichter, *The Strategy of Desire* (Boardman, 1958)

James Dyson, *Against The Odds: An autobiography* (Texere, 2000)

Alan Fletcher, *The Art of Looking Sideways* (Phaidon, 2001)

Michael E. Gerber, *The E Myth Revisited: Why most small businesses don't work and what to do about it* (HarperCollins, 1994)

John Grant, *The New Marketing Manifesto: The 12 rules for building successful brands in the 21st century* (Texere, 2000)

Michael Maccoby, *The Productive Narcissist: The Promise and Peril of Visionary Leadership* (Broadway Books, 2003)

Christopher Vogler, *The Writer's Journey: Mythic Structure for Writers* (Pan, 1999)

Shoshana Zuboff and James Maxmin, *The Support Economy: Why corporations are failing individuals and the next episode of capitalism* (Penguin, 2004)